FOR JOE —

HAPPY BIRTHDAY 00

HAPPY + HUNTING c°°

Our love to you.

Richard D°

SANTA BARBARA COUNTY

JANET PENN FRANKS

CENTRAL COAST PRESS

San Luis Obispo, California

ISBN10: 1-930401-57-4
ISBN13: 978-1-930401-57-0

Printed in China

CENTRAL COAST PRESS
P.O. Box 3654
San Luis Obispo, California

Distributor:
PACIFIC BOOKS
P.O. Box 3562
Santa Barbara, California 93130

Wineries featured in this book were chosen because they provided wine tasting without appointments, their locations were of particular interest to visitors, and they were in regular operation at press time. All photography is by Janet Penn Franks, except where noted. For more information about this book and the author and how to purchase photographs, see **www.janetpennfranks.com**. For information about Central Coast Press, see **www.centralcoastbooks.com**.

DEDICATION

This book is dedicated to my children, Allison and Erik.

Cambria Estate Vineyards & Winery, Santa Maria

CONTENTS

PART ONE: SANTA BARBARA COUNTY WINERIES

PART TWO: MORE WINE-TASTING VENUES

ACKNOWLEDGMENTS

I would like to thank the members of the Santa Barbara County wine community, who took the time to share information with me about their wineries.

I would also like to express my particular appreciation to Catherine Cavaletto (owner, San Jose Winery), for sharing her historic winery with me; to Fran Clow (executive administrator, Santa Barbara County Vintners' Association), for her knowledge of Santa Barbara County AVAs; to Lynn Diehl (owner, Lynn Diehl Media), who suggested I write this book and gave me her steadfast support; to Gere and Laura di Zerega, for their support and encouragement and for the publishing expertise that Laura shared with me; to Alec Franks (winemaker, Rancho Sisquoc Winery), for a photo-shoot jeep ride; to Nels and Vicki Hanson (Hanson Editing), for editorial support; to Craig Jaffurs (owner, Jaffurs Wine Cellars) and Jan Wolfinger (Jan Wolfinger Graphic Design, Inc.), for their photographs; to Lee Anne Fisher, Margo Fraser, Kathleen Karle, and Vicki Pobor, who encouraged me throughout this project; to Doug Margerum (owner and winemaker, Margerum Wine Company/ Wine Cask), for supplying extra recipes; and to the Santa Barbara County Historical Society, for providing historical photos.

Special gratitude goes to my family: to my husband, John, my "unofficial" business advisor and wine guru, for his invaluable suggestions, his continued patience during the writing of another book, and his companionship on wine-tasting trips in Santa Barbara County; to my children, Allison and Erik, for their support; and to my sister, Laura Penn Harmon, and brother-in-law, Dave Harmon, for their unwavering enthusiasm.

Lincourt Vinyards, Solvang

Pages 4-5: Spring wildflowers at Rusack Vineyards, Solvang
Page 7: Cattle graze across the road from Zaca Mesa's vineyards in the Santa Ynez Valley

A NOTE FROM THE AUTHOR

Thank you for your interest in **Santa Barbara County Wineries**. This book is intended to guide you through the county's many wine-tasting venues. From small artisan wineries to large-scale production establishments, Santa Barbara County has a wine-tasting destination for everyone. Several local wine shops and an inn also offer wine tasting from a variety of Santa Barbara County wineries that do not maintain their own tasting rooms.

For current wine ratings and accolades, please visit individual winery Web sites and/or refer to *Wine Spectator*, *Robert M. Parker, Jr.'s The Wine Advocate*, and *Wine Enthusiast* magazines.

Wine tasting is a personal experience. I encourage you to explore the wine country's back roads and stroll the streets of Santa Barbara, Solvang, Los Olivos, Santa Ynez, and Los Alamos to find a comfortable place to sit, sip, and savor what Santa Barbara County has to offer.

Enjoy!

Janet Penn Franks

THE HISTORY OF WINEMAKING
IN SANTA BARBARA COUNTY

More than 200 years ago Santa Barbara County's world-renowned wine country was first planted with grapevines. Among the early plantings, two cuttings lived to an astonishingly old age and grew to enormous, legendary size. Known as *La Parra Grande* and *La Vina Grande*, the famous grapevines produced fruit in great abundance for almost a century in the region's rich soil, warm climate, and cool Pacific breezes.

The thick-trunked, trellised grapevines reached wider than the limbs of the largest tree, providing shade for community meetings and celebrations attended by Franciscan priests from Spain, Mexican soldiers and ranchers and their wives and children, an Irish immigrant fresh from the gold fields of the Mother Lode country, a wine-loving judge born in Rhode Island, and two star-crossed lovers pursuing romance against the wishes of stern, Old World parents—

These long-departed Californians—and a crew of marauding, Pacific Ocean pirates in 19th-century sailing ships—number among the many vivid figures who are part of Santa Barbara County's rich winemaking history.

The legend of *La Parra Grande* ("The Great Grapevine") began about 1780, after Marcelina Feliz, a beautiful Spanish girl living near Los Angeles, fell in love with José Dominguez, who was handsome, intelligent, and poor. To thwart the young lovers' romance, Marcelina's mother and father decided to move with their daughter to Montecito, just south of Santa Barbara.

The night before the Feliz family's departure, at a final secret tryst, José asked Marcelina to remain true to him for two years, and gave her a shoot from a Mission grapevine, telling her to plant it beside her new home.

When Marcelina arrived in Montecito she planted the vine and it grew with amazing vigor and speed, as if nourished by the power of Marcelina and José's love. Two years later Señor Feliz arranged a marriage between Marcelina and an old but wealthy *don*. On the eve of the wedding, a distraught Marcelina took refuge under the sheltering canopy of José's grapevine. José heard of the impending marriage and hurried from Los Angeles to Montecito, where he found Marcelina weeping by his flourishing vine. He announced that he had made a fortune mining gold, and once again asked Señor Feliz for his daughter's hand. Señor Feliz gave his permission, and Marcelina and José were married the next day.

La Parra Grande grew to a circumference of four and a half feet and its canes completely covered its 5,000-square-foot arbor. The massive vine produced 16,000 pounds of grapes per year and was a Montecito gathering place until 1876, when the dying vine was cut down and shipped to the Midwest for a centennial celebration.

In Carpinteria, just south of Montecito, a grapevine that became known as *La Vina Grande* ("The Great Vine") grew to even greater proportions. In 1842, Señora Lugo de

Louisa Dominguez, the daughter of José Dominguez and Marcelina Feliz Dominguez, beneath *La Parra Grande*, Montecito, c. 1870
(*Photo courtesy Santa Barbara Historical Society*)

Ayala planted a Mission-variety cutting beside her home—the vine rapidly climbed its nine-foot trellis and at maturity its twisting trunk measured nearly 10 feet around and its vast canopy spread across a half-acre arbor.

La Vina Grande produced 10 tons of fruit per year in bunches that weighed as much as 22 pounds. In 1893, organizers of the Chicago World's Fair offered $1,000 for *La Vina Grande,* but Jacob Wilson, its new owner, declined and the Great Vine lived on until the 1920s.

La Vina Grande, Carpinteria, c. 1900
(Photo courtesy Santa Barbara Historical Society)

FRANCISCAN WINEMAKERS

A religious expedition brought the first winemakers to California in the late 1700s, when the King of Spain sent Franciscan padres to colonize Alta California in the far northern corner of Spanish Mexico and to convert local Indians to Christianity.

Between 1769 and 1823, the Franciscans established a chain of 21 missions, each within a day's walk from the next, along *El Camino Real* ("The Royal Road"), which followed the California coastline. Missions Santa Barbara, La Purísima Concepción, and Santa Inés were founded in what later became Santa Barbara County.

Spanish explorers in the 1500s had found several indigenous species of grapes along the coast, but the native fruit was small, seedy, and sour, and unsuited for wine production. The padres at the Santa Barbara County missions became the region's first growers of wine grapes when they planted the *Vitis vinifera* vines—known as the "Mission" variety—propagated from cuttings brought from Europe to the New World by Father Junipero Serra.

The father of California winemaking, Serra led efforts to plant grapevines to supply wine for communion, and vineyards were growing at each California mission within 10 years of its founding.

In 1786, Father Fermin de Lasuen founded Mission Santa Barbara three miles from the Pacific Ocean, on a hillside that offered a view of a wooded valley and the Channel Islands. By 1800, the Santa Barbara padres were making wine for religious services from grapes grown on the mission grounds and in their three main vineyards: San Jose in present-day Goleta, Vina Aroya in Mission Canyon, and La Cieneguita at the south end of San Marcos Pass.

The unstinting labor of Chumash Indians allowed Santa Barbara to become the second most productive wine producer among the California missions. At first, grapes were crushed by foot, until mission coopers built simple, screw-type presses.

The Mission grape yielded a sweet, harsh-tasting red wine that mellowed slightly when allowed to mature. Unfortunately, the grape's low level of tannic acid usually caused the wine to turn to vinegar before it could age

The vineyard at Mission Santa Barbara, c. 1909
(Photo courtesy Santa Barbara Historical Society)

sufficiently. An inadequate supply of barrels, especially white oak barrels the Franciscans had used in Europe, also hindered proper aging.

"If you have any empty barrels, send them," reads a 1797 letter sent by one padre to a Baja California supplier. Communications among missions and with early secular wine buyers included urgent requests for the return of empty barrels.

Like European winemakers who produced brandy from poor-quality wine, the Franciscans built stills and converted much of their wine into *aguardiente*, a 150-proof brandy.

In 1787, Father de Lasuen established Mission La Purísima Concepción near the future site of the city of Lompoc. One of the most prosperous missions, La Purísima Concepción harvested grapes from its two vineyards, which thrived in the region's fertile valley. Mission Santa Inés was founded in 1804 by Father Estevan Tapis and is located in Solvang, 35 miles northeast of Santa Barbara. Santa Inés padres planted grapevines on the mission's grounds and three vineyards in nearby areas know as Refugio, Tajiguas, and Arroyo Hondo.

A metal sculpture of Father Junipero Serra and an early El Camino Real bell, Mission Santa Barbara, 2006

SECULAR VINEYARDS

The art of winemaking in Santa Barbara County soon spread to early settlers who sought suitable climates, terrains, and grape varieties for making wine and brandy.

In 1794, the José Francisco Ortega family established one of the region's first secular, privately owned vineyards on a plot of land adjacent to modern-day Goleta along the Pacific coast. Governor Diego Borico granted the land to the family, with the stipulation that they plant a vineyard, an orchard, and grains and vegetables at the mouth of Refugio Canyon.

The Ortega family's seaside settlement became known as Rancho Nuestra Señora del Refugio ("Our Lady of Refuge Ranch") and for a good while the Ortegas prospered as purveyors of wine, brandy, and fresh produce. But when several Ortega brothers sharecropped grapes for the nearby Mission La Purísima Concepción, local homesteaders became suspicious. Neighboring settlers believed the brothers were involved in illegal activities and that they'd made irregular arrangements with the mission and served as confidential agents for the padres.

By the early 1800s, the Ortegas' Rancho Refugio and its wharf had acquired a reputation as a smuggling port for trading vessels, where both goods and foreigners could come ashore undetected. But it was the rumor of a treasure stored at Rancho Refugio that brought about the downfall of one of Santa Barbara County's first winemaking families.

In 1818, Captain Hippolyte de Bouchard of Argentina, who commanded two pirate ships in the waters off California's coast, heard news of the Ortega "treasure." Captain Bouchard planned to assault the Ortegas after striking the residents of Monterey 240 miles to the north.

Word of the pirate's imminent attack reached Rancho Refugio and other coastal ranchos and pueblos. Property owners moved family members, children, and livestock inland and prepared to defend their homesteads.

In early December, Bouchard's ships arrived at the Ortega wharf. Within 24 hours, the captain and his men had plundered and set fire to the ranch buildings and sailed off with the spoils of their devastating raid. In the years after the attack, the Ortegas rebuilt their nearly destroyed settlement but never regained their former prosperity.

Rancho Refugio had been an easy target, even though Spanish authorities in 1782 had constructed a *presidio* ("fort") in Santa

Barbara to protect ranchos, pueblos, mining camps, and friendly Indians, and promote the occupation of new territory. For the Ortegas, the proximity of the *presidio* had made little difference, but for two of the *presidio*'s commanders the immediate area's rich soils and mild, favorable climate offered an opportunity to become successful vintners.

Comandante Felipe de Goycoechea became a wine grower in 1843 when he planted a vineyard on land that is today bounded by Carrillo, Anapamu, Castillo, and De la Vina streets in downtown Santa Barbara.

And by 1860 Comandante José Antonio de la Guerra y Noriega was producing nearly 6,000 gallons of wine a year from a local vineyard. Noriega's assistant and neighbor, Don Gaspar de Orena, also made wine near the *presidio* at his family's winery, which remained in business until the early 20th century. The Orena family's small adobe still stands on the corner of De la Guerra and Anacapa streets in downtown Santa Barbara.

With a military flavor, the commercial wine industry of Santa Barbara County was well under way—and soon would grow larger and more lucrative with the emergence of two ambitious, English-speaking newcomers.

In the late 1850s, Judge Albert Packard, a Rhode Island native, purchased 200 acres on the west side of Santa Barbara and planted a large vineyard. Sometime after 1865, the judge constructed the city's first major winery, the huge three-story *La Bodega* ("The Wine Cellar"), on West Carrillo Street.

The judge bottled wine, including claret—his specialty—and labeled his vintages *"El Recedo"* ("The Corner"). Each year, with the assistance of several winemakers, Packard made nearly 9,000 gallons of wine, which he shipped to Los Angeles, San Luis Obispo, and markets as distant as Texas.

One of Santa Barbara County's early winemaking establishments, the San Jose Winery in Goleta, was leased in 1859 by James McCaffery, an Irish immigrant and a veteran of the California Gold Rush. The tile-roofed adobe winery had been built by Mission Santa Barbara several decades earlier, and McCaffery took up the padres' winemaking methods as he labored in the winery and farmed the 2,200 grapevines, irrigating the vineyard with water from nearby San Jose Creek. McCaffery purchased the property in 1871 and within six years had increased the vineyard to 6,700 vines.

(After McCaffery's death in 1900, Michele Cavaletto bought the vineyard and winery and his family made wine there until Prohibition. The Cavalettos later enclosed the historic adobe with a metal-roofed wood structure to preserve the padres' original working quarters from the elements. Although the San Jose vineyard disappeared long ago, the venerable winery remains Goleta's oldest existing building and still houses the original fermentation vat and winemaking tools.)

While winemaking flourished in Santa Barbara County in the second half of the 19th century, the European wine industry was experiencing an agricultural catastrophe that would bring Continental wines to California.

In the 1860s, '70s, and '80s, an epidemic of phylloxera—a leaf and root parasite that American vines were resistant to—ravaged the vineyards of France and large areas of Europe. But before the French could replant their fields with rootstock immune to the

The adobe home of mid-19th-century winemaker Don Gaspar de Orena, corner of De la Guerra and Anacapa streets in downtown Santa Barbara, 2006

The historic San Jose Winery, Goleta, 2006

parasite, they needed to save their classic varietals. The French ministry of agriculture asked many French immigrants living in the Western Hemisphere to accept cuttings from the afflicted French vines and graft them onto the hardy Mission rootstock.

The winegrowing disaster in the Old World spurred Santa Barbara County vintners to begin growing European varietals.

French-born Justinian Claire founded Santa Cruz Island Winery in the 1880s. Twenty-five miles off the shore of Carpinteria, Santa Barbara County's best-known and most successful pre-Prohibition winery produced record-breaking quantities of wine that included several varietals from his homeland.

Claire had immigrated in 1851 to San Francisco, where he established a successful hardware business and served on the board of directors of a French bank. In 1869, Claire and his fellow board members purchased the 96-square-mile Santa Cruz Island, which was then one of California's largest sheep ranches.

The enterprising Claire bought out his partners in 1880 and sailed to the island, where he started a variety of farming, ranching, and construction projects, including the building of numerous structures and outbuildings and a narrow-gauge railroad that ran from his ranch house to his wharf. Claire established fruit orchards and raised fields of vegetables and alfalfa hay.

In 1884, Claire began his most ambitious operation when he planted more than 200 acres of Zinfandel, Cabernet Franc, Cabernet Sauvignon, Barbera, Pinot Noir, Grenache, Muscat, Riesling, Burger, Chasselas, and Sauvignon Vert vines in the island's central valley.

Santa Cruz Winery's first wines were made in the small, wood-framed beekeeper's house.

The grape press used by winemaker Michele Cavaletto, San Jose Winery, Goleta, 2006

Later, on the crest of a hill, Claire constructed a larger winery made of island-clay bricks. Claire's winemakers crushed grapes and fermented juice in the winery's upper level and let gravity transport the wine to the cellar, where it aged in barrels before shipment to San Francisco for bottling. Claire sold his Santa Cruz Island wines to customers in both Los Angeles and San Francisco.

By the 1890s, Santa Cruz Island Winery was producing more than 25,000 gallons of wine per year, and 83,000 gallons by 1910. In 1918, the winery made its last vintage before Prohibition ended commercial winemaking in Santa Barbara County for more than a decade.

The original fermentation vat and wine barrels remain at the San Jose Winery, Goleta, 2006

PROHIBITION

At the beginning of the 20th century, California was the United States' leading wine producer—the vintages of Golden State wine growers accounted for 88 percent of the domestic wine market.

And California winemakers needed to be productive—in 1913, America's yearly wine consumption had reached a third of a gallon per person, establishing a national market for 50 million gallons of wine a year.

As American wine production and consumption increased, the Temperance Movement gained momentum, rallying the public against alcohol and lobbying the government for the banning of beer, wine, and spirits. Congress passed the Volstead Act in 1919 and the law went into effect in 1920, outlawing the manufacture, sale, and transportation of alcoholic beverages in the United States.

Although the ban on alcohol devastated the Santa Barbara County wine industry, a number of commercial county vintners ignored the law, continuing to make wine in their basements and other clandestine locations. When Prohibition ended in 1933, many "underground" winemaking operations became bonded wineries.

A NEW BEGINNING

Santa Barbara County winemaking experienced a rebirth in the 1960s and '70s with the founding of several wineries that flourished and today offer premium wines to 21st-century wine enthusiasts.

In 1962, Canadian-born architect Pierre Lafond established Santa Barbara Winery, the first commercial winery in the county since the end of Prohibition. Lafond, who had moved in the late 1950s to Santa Barbara to run his family's downtown liquor store, began making "affordable" wine from purchased grapes from San Luis Obispo County and Northern California. After discovering he could make exceptional wine with fruit grown in Santa Barbara County, Lafond purchased his own vineyard in the Santa Rita Hills in 1972. He planted another vineyard in the 1990s and launched a second label, Lafond Winery & Vineyard.

Northeast of Lafond's Santa Barbara Winery, Santa Maria Valley wine-growing pioneers Uriel Nielson and Bill De Mattei developed a portion of the historic 9,000-acre Rancho Tepusquet into an important wine-growing area.

Nielson and De Mattei were friends and both viticulture graduates of the University of California, Davis. In the early 1960s they began conducting studies to determine the most suitable grape-growing soil and climate in Santa Barbara County and purchased approximately 100 acres east of Santa Maria, land that was part of the original Rancho Tepusquet grant from the Mexican government.

The fertile soil of the Santa Maria Bench on Rancho Tepusquet is ideal for growing grapes.

In 1964 the partners planted the county's first post-Prohibition vineyard on "The Bench," the raised, level track of fertile Rancho Tepusquet land just north of the Sisquoc River.

The 30-acre Nielson Vineyard comprised Chardonnay, Sauvignon Blanc, Cabernet Sauvignon, Sylvaner, and Riesling vines. Four years later, when the grapes were ready for harvest, the Christian Brothers Winery in Napa Valley offered Nielson and De Mattei a five-year contract, agreeing to purchase their fruit at a price above the then-current market rate.

News of Nielson and De Mattei's successful grape-growing venture traveled fast. The September 30, 1969, edition of the *Santa Barbara News-Press* heralded "Santa Barbara County's newest and perhaps most glamorous crop" and declared the microclimate at Rancho Tepusquet "ideal for grapes."

In 1969, Croatian-born brothers Louis and George Lucas—fourth-generation table-grape farmers who lived in the San Joaquin Valley—purchased 1,300 acres of the old Rancho and established their Tepusquet Vineyard.

For three decades, the brothers sold grapes to premier Northern California wineries, but by the mid-1990s Louis wanted to make his own wine. He asked his friend, retired Superior Court Judge Royce Lewellen, to become a co-partner in establishing a winery. The two men founded Lucas & Lewellen Vineyards & Winery in 1996 and Mandolina Winery in 2002.

The same year that the Lucas brothers established their Tepusquet Vineyard, the Miller family purchased 800 acres in the western part of Rancho Tepusquet, near the rancho's original 1857 adobe that stands today.

The Millers named their vineyard property "Bien Nacido" ("Well Born") to describe the land's rich soil that grows prized grapes. One of Santa Barbara County's outstanding vineyards, Bien Nacido sells its coveted fruit to respected California wineries.

Santa Barbara County's grape-growing industry had begun to revive at the beginning of the 1960s—many farmers began to convert grazing land into vineyards, raising high-quality harvests that brought unprecedented returns from large, Northern California wineries.

Cattle rancher and farmer James Flood owned the historic 37,000-acre Rancho Sisquoc, located just south of the Sisquoc River, in the northeastern portion of the Santa Maria Valley. Flood wanted to join the burgeoning wine industry, and in preparation for becoming a grape grower he irrigated a portion of his grazing land that lay on the south bank of the Sisquoc River. Two years later, in 1970, he planted a vineyard with Cabernet Sauvignon and Johannisberg Riesling.

Flood intended to grow and sell his fruit to wineries in Northern California, but in the early 1970s ranch manager Harold Pfeiffer began to experiment, making small batches of wine. In 1977, Flood founded Rancho Sisquoc Winery in a small wood structure that now serves as the winery's tasting room.

WINE GROWERS TO WINEMAKERS

During the 1970s, a multitude of wineries began to spring up next to established vineyards as many Santa Barbara County grape growers now also became winemakers. The sudden expansion of local winemaking was caused by several immediate and sometimes apparently contradictory factors.

County viticulturists realized that their grapes were of exceptional quality and were producing award-winning wines for Northern California vintners. Why sell and send prize fruit to the north, when excellent, highly profitable wine could be made at county wineries?

The wine boom in northern Santa Barbara County spurred a rising real estate market for land that could produce premium, lucrative wine grapes—rural property owners had a strong incentive to market their properties as potential vineyard sites. Land sales and vine plantings were increasing and new, local wineries could expect a steady supply of fruit.

And, oddly enough, county wineries grew in number as a result of the national recession during the early 1970s. The economic downturn caused a decrease in national wine consumption, and therefore a decline in the amount of Santa Barbara County grapes purchased by Northern California wineries. Faced with an oversupply and declining prices for their fruit, local growers turned to winemaking to market their surplus grapes and as an insurance policy against future economic hardships.

As the media and enthusiastic critics continued to acclaim locally made wines and describe a bright future for Santa Barbara County winemaking, the local wine industry grew exponentially. Wine growing became an alluring and exciting enterprise, not only to people with viticulture or general farming backgrounds, but also to wine aficionados who worked in a wide range of other professions.

In 1971, Lompoc dentist Bill Mosby and his wife, Geraldine, took the advice of Robert Gallo, Bill's fraternity brother, and planted eight acres of wine grapes on Santa Rosa Road, on the north bank of the Santa Ynez River. Mosby converted an old barn on the property for winemaking and established Mosby Winery.

That same year, geographer Richard Sanford and botanist Michael Benedict purchased a 700-acre bean and cattle farm on Santa Rosa Road, just west of the Mosbys' vineyard. They planted their Sanford & Benedict Vineyard with the intent of making their own wine, which is sold today under the Sanford Winery & Vineyards label.

Leonard Firestone, an ambassador to Belgium and the son of tire magnate Harvey Firestone, established vines in the early 1970s on the family's Santa Ynez Valley cattle ranch. Like many other growers, Firestone had at first planned to sell his grapes to Northern California wineries, but now his son, Brooks, left his position at Firestone Tire and Rubber Company to take part in the family's new venture. The younger Firestone wasn't content to sell grapes to other wineries, and began research into wine and winemaking. In 1972, Brooks Firestone founded the region's first estate winery and visitor center, producing Firestone Vineyard's premiere vintage in 1975.

YESTERDAY, TODAY, AND TOMORROW

By the end of the 1970s, Santa Barbara County winemakers had already earned an honored place on the international wine scene, winning accolades in prestigious wine competitions and special notice in the worldwide media.

And as the 1970s became the 1980s, local wine growing had evolved into more than simply growing grapes and making wine. Wine tasting had become a popular pastime and an important part of the county's tourist industry—by car, Santa Barbara County is only an hour and a half from Los Angeles and that city's international airport.

As the popularity of Santa Barbara County's wines continued to grow, increasing numbers of discriminating wine lovers arrived each year to sample local vintages in the county's charming tasting rooms, and to visit prizewinning vineyards set amid the spectacular rural scenery of Old California. Several large wineries—including Gainey Vineyard, Fess Parker Winery & Vineyard, and Zaca Mesa Winery & Vineyards—constructed spacious and comfortable visitor-friendly tasting rooms, where special gatherings and events could be held.

As of 2005, 16,597 acres of wine grapes had been planted in Santa Barbara County and the annual grape crush had reached 125,418 tons, an enormous quantity, especially when compared to the harvests of Father Serra's vineyards.

As visitors to Santa Barbara's wine country lift their glasses of handcrafted vintages, they continue to enjoy a tradition that began with the Old Californians who once sat among friends, beneath the shading leaves of *La Parra Grande* and *La Vina Grande*, and drank the wine that each year was made from the arbors' generous bounty.

SANTA BARBARA COUNTY
SUB-AVAs

Santa Maria Valley

Santa Ynez Valley

Santa Rita Hills

Happy Canyon

SANTA MARIA

ORCUTT

LOS ALAMOS

Los Alamos Valley

LOMPOC

BUELLTON

LOS OLIVOS

SANTA YNEZ

Ballard Canyon

SOLVANG

GOLETA

SANTA BARBARA

A FEW WORDS ABOUT AVAs

No two vineyards are exactly alike.

Natural conditions specific to geographic location—altitude, soil, topography, sun, rain, fog, and wind—give every vineyard and the wine it produces characteristics as unique as a fingerprint.

And yet the prints from a single hand bear a close resemblance, as do wines produced in similar locales.

Grape-growing areas with the same geographic conditions are referred to as "appellations of origin." However, Europeans and Americans define "appellation" differently.

In Europe, an appellation refers to a place name—Burgundy, Bordeaux, Rhône Valley, for example—*and* also describes a style of wine. European governments regulate which grape varieties may be planted in each appellation and which cultivation methods and winemaking techniques may be used there. The purpose of European appellations is to ensure that every bottle of wine bottled under a particular appellation conforms to the authentic wine style of that region.

In the United States, the appellation of origin refers to the country, state, county, or American Viticulture Area (AVA) where the grapes were grown. The AVA system was designated in 1978 by the Alcohol and Tobacco Tax and Trade Bureau (formerly the Bureau of Alcohol, Tobacco, and Firearms) to identify "official" grape-growing regions. AVA appellations are used to regulate *only* the geographic boundaries of the growing areas—each winery is free to choose the grape varieties it plants and the manner of cultivation.

American appellations help consumers better identify the wines they purchase and aid winemakers in distinguishing their products from wines made in other areas. When an AVA is designated on a wine bottle's label, at least 85 percent of the wine must come from that AVA.

As of August 2006, there were 182 AVAs in the United States, 106 of them located in California. The Central Coast AVA, established in 1985, covers approximately 1 million acres and includes parts of Monterey, Santa Cruz, Santa Clara, Alameda, San Benito, San Luis Obispo, and Santa Barbara counties.

An AVA can contain smaller sub-AVAs. Santa Barbara County has three official sub-AVAs—Santa Maria Valley, Santa Ynez Valley, and Santa Rita Hills—and three "unofficial" sub-AVAs—Los Alamos, Happy Canyon, and Ballard Canyon. (The place names "Los Alamos," "Happy Canyon," and "Ballard Canyon" do not appear on wine labels. Wines made from grapes grown in these regions are labeled "Santa Barbara County.")

Santa Ynez Valley, Santa Rita Hills, Los Alamos, Happy Canyon, and Ballard Canyon lie in the central part of Santa Barbara County, while Santa Maria Valley lies in the north.

A portion of the Sisquoc River winds its way past the vineyards of Rancho Sisquoc Winery in the Santa Maria Valley.

The Santa Maria Valley Sub-AVA

Established in 1981, the Santa Maria Valley sub-AVA encompasses more than 97,000 acres. The majority of the region lies in Santa Barbara County, while the small northern section lies in San Luis Obispo County.

The alluvial soil of the Santa Maria Valley was deposited by the Santa Maria and the Sisquoc rivers and is mainly sandy loam with areas of clay loam and pure sand.

Situated in an east/west-oriented valley, the Santa Maria Valley sub-AVA is bordered on the northeast by the Los Padres National Forest and the San Rafael Mountains, on the southwest by the Solomon Hills, and on the northwest by the city of Santa Maria, which is 18 miles from the Pacific Ocean. Marine air sweeps inland between the cities of Grover Beach and Guadalupe to the Santa Maria Valley, causing the climate of this sub-AVA to remain cool year round.

The combination of Pacific breezes and both fog and ample sunshine creates one of California's longest grape-growing seasons. These climatic conditions allow for an unusually long "hang time," so the grapes ripen fully before harvest. The marine influence is especially favorable to the production of Chardonnay and Pinot Noir, the flagship varietals of this sub-AVA.

The Santa Ynez Valley Sub-AVA

The Santa Ynez Valley sub-AVA lies south of the Santa Maria Valley. Established in 1983, it encompasses more than 180,000 acres of varied soils, including sandy clay, gravely loams, and well-drained benchlands.

Situated on an east/west axis, the Santa Ynez Valley is bordered on the north by the Santa Maria Valley, on the south by the Santa Ynez Mountains, on the east by the San Rafael Mountains, on the west by the city of Lompoc, and farther west by the Pacific Ocean. The Santa Ynez River flows through the southern part of the region.

Warmer than the Santa Maria sub-AVA, the Santa Ynez sub-AVA contains both warm and cool microclimates that allow the cultivation of a diversity of grapes—Syrah, Cabernet Sauvignon, Merlot, Grenache, and Sauvignon Blanc, to name a few. Sea air blows from the north and the west, making the northwest portion of the Santa Ynez sub-AVA the coolest. The warmest climates are found in the valley's center, near the town of Los Olivos, and in the easternmost area.

Because of the variety of climates and soil types, the Santa Ynez Valley sub-AVA contains four separate sub-districts, only one of which is officially recognized—the Santa Rita Hills.

The Santa Rita Hills Sub-AVA

The Santa Rita Hills sub-AVA lies within the western portion of the Santa Ynez sub-AVA and covers more than 33,000 acres. Santa Rita Hills was officially established in 2001 to distinguish the cool, western region of the Santa Ynez Valley from the warmer, eastern part. (In 2006, "Santa Rita Hills," the sub-AVA's original designation, was legally abbreviated to "Sta. Rita Hills" to avoid confusion with a Chilean winery, Viña Santa Rita.)

This sub-AVA is located approximately three miles east of Lompoc and five miles west of Highway 101. It straddles the winding Santa Ynez River and is bordered on the north by the La Purisima Hills, on the south by the Santa Rosa Hills, on the east by the Santa Ynez Valley sub-AVA, and on the west by the city of Lompoc. The Santa Rita sub-AVA spans approximately 15 miles from east to west.

Santa Rita Hills differs from the rest of the Santa Ynez sub-AVA in both climate and soils. Early-morning fog and the strong, afternoon Pacific breezes that blow through the hilly terrain create optimal conditions for Pinot Noir and Chardonnay grapes. The soils are predominately dune sand with areas of sandy loam, Monterey shale, Botella clay loam, and alluvial gravel. Calcareous material, including marl and chalk, is intermixed in many of the soils.

Home to pioneering wineries such as Sanford, Lafond, and Babcock, the Santa Rita Hills sub-AVA is one of California's top Pinot Noir growing regions.

The Los Alamos Valley

Although the Los Alamos Valley has not been designated as an official viticultural area, it is widely considered to be a unique wine-growing region.

The valley contains approximately 5,600 acres of vines—the grapes are primarily Chardonnay and Pinot Noir, with smaller acreages planted to Italian varieties.

Soils are mostly clay loam, similar to those found in the eastern Santa Ynez Valley.

Early-morning fog lingers at El Camino Vineyard, Los Alamos.

Bounded on the north by the Solomon Hills and on the south by the La Purisima Hills, the Los Alamos region straddles Highway 101. Most of the vineyards are planted east of the highway.

The Los Alamos Valley draws cool air and fog inland from the Pacific Ocean. On average, the climate is 10 degrees warmer than in the Santa Maria Valley and 10 degrees cooler than in the Santa Ynez Valley.

Happy Canyon and Ballard Canyon

Happy Canyon and Ballard Canyon are unofficial viticulture areas that lie within the Santa Ynez Valley-sub AVA.

The Happy Canyon region is located in the warmest, easternmost part of the Santa Ynez Valley, where temperatures average approximately 10 degrees warmer than in Los Olivos. Bordeaux and Rhône varietals thrive in this area, which encompasses about 250 acres.

Ballard Canyon lies in the central part of the Santa Ynez Valley, between Los Olivos and Solvang. Elevations are mixed— hilltop plantings are cooled by ocean breezes while low-lying vineyards grow in warmer temperatures. The terrain varies from calcareous soil to sand or sandy loam.

HOW TO READ A WINE LABEL

Winery/Brand Name — Au Bon Climat

Vintage — 20 04

Place of Origin

Vineyard Name — LE BON CLIMAT

Santa Maria Valley
PINOT NOIR

Type of Wine

Produced and bottled by Jim Clendenen, Mind Behind
Santa Maria, California, B.W. 5107, from grapes grown at
Le Bon Climat Vineyard.   Alcohol 13.5% by volume.

Alcohol Content

DEFINITION OF WINE TERMS

In the United States, the **name of the winery** that made the wine or the **brand name** is prominently displayed on the label.

The **vintage** is the year the grapes were harvested, not the year the wine was released. At least 95 percent of the wine in a bottle must come from grapes harvested in the year printed on the label.

The **vineyard name** usually indicates that the wine was made from grapes from an exceptional vineyard. At least 95 percent of a vineyard-designated wine must be made from the vineyard named on the label.

The **type of wine** usually indicates the grape variety or varieties used to make the wine.

The **place of origin** identifies the place where the grapes were grown, and does not necessarily denote where the wine was made. A state name—California, for example—indicates that 100 percent of the wine came from grapes grown within the state. An AVA or sub-AVA name means that at least 85 percent of the wine's grapes came from that specific appellation. A county name means that at least 75 percent of the wine's grapes were grown within the county.

The **alcohol content** is the percentage of alcohol in the wine, which usually ranges between 7 and 17 percent.

Other information sometimes found on the label is the description **"Estate bottled,"** which means the winery owns and controls the vineyard where the grapes were grown.

"Reserve" wines are those deemed finer than the normal version of the winery's same wine.

The Alcohol and Tobacco Tax and Trade Bureau requires the **bottle's net contents** to be displayed in milliliters. Standard-size bottles are 750 ml and splits are 350 ml.

The bottle's **back label** displays information about the wine, which may include the vineyard in which the grapes were grown, winemaking techniques, and tips on food pairing. Mandatory information includes the government warning by the surgeon general stating the health effects of alcohol (including impairment in operating machinery) and a "contains sulfites" warning if appropriate.

Photo above: Before harvest at a vineyard on Foxen Canyon Road

Photo below: After harvest at the same Foxen Canyon vineyard

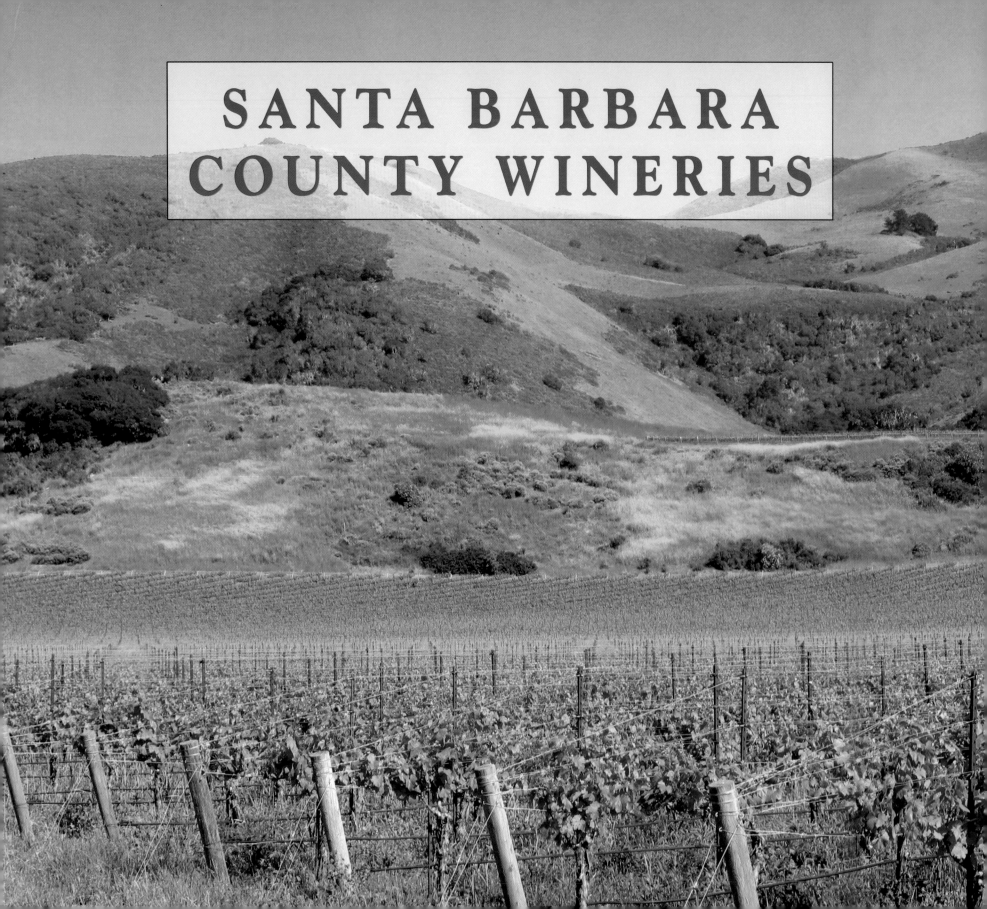

SANTA BARBARA
COUNTY WINERIES

Santa Maria Valley fall foliage

Pages 24-25: Rancho La Rinconada Vineyard, Sanford Winery & Vineyards, Buellton

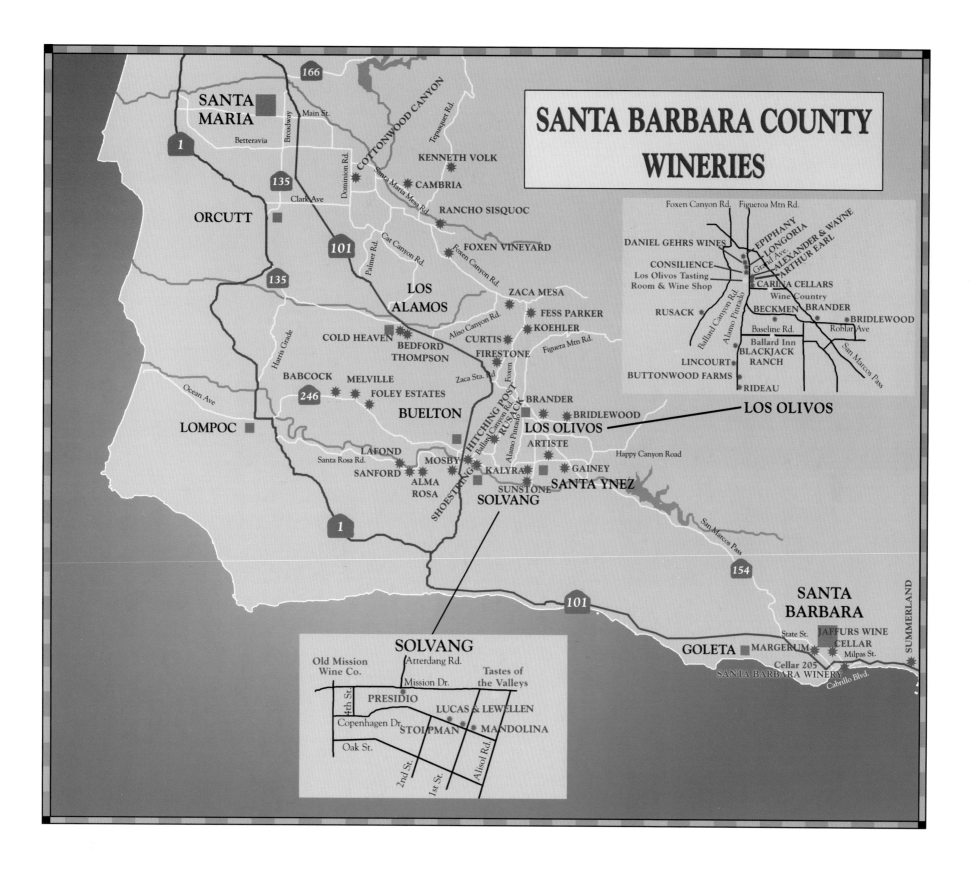

SANTA BARBARA COUNTY WINERIES

SANTA MARIA

Main St.
Betteravia
Broadway
166
1
135
Clark Ave
Dominion Rd.
Palmer Rd.
Cat Canyon Rd.
Santa Maria Mesa Rd.
Tepusquet Rd.

COTTONWOOD CANYON

KENNETH VOLK
CAMBRIA
RANCHO SISQUOC

ORCUTT

101
135

FOXEN VINEYARD
Foxen Canyon Rd.

LOS ALAMOS

ZACA MESA
FESS PARKER
KOEHLER

Harris Grade

COLD HEAVEN
BEDFORD THOMPSON
Aliso Canyon Rd.
CURTIS
FIRESTONE
Figuera Mtn Rd.

BABCOCK
MELVILLE
FOLEY ESTATES
Zaca Sta. Rd.

Ocean Ave
246

BUELTON

BRANDER
BRIDLEWOOD
LOS OLIVOS
ARTISTE

LOMPOC
1

LAFOND
Santa Rosa Rd.
SANFORD
ALMA ROSA
MOSBY
KALYRA
SUNSTONE
GAINEY
Happy Canyon Road
SANTA YNEZ

HITCHING POST
RUSACK
SHOESTRING
Ballard Canyon Rd.
Alamo Pintado
Foxen

SOLVANG

San Marcos Pass

154

101

SANTA BARBARA

GOLETA
State St.
MARGERUM
JAFFURS WINE CELLAR
Milpas St.
Cellar 205
SANTA BARBARA WINERY
Cabrillo Blvd.
SUMMERLAND

LOS OLIVOS

Foxen Canyon Rd.   Figueroa Mtn Rd.

DANIEL GEHRS WINES
EPIPHANY
LONGORIA
ALEXANDER & WAYNE
ARTHUR EARL
CONSILIENCE
Los Olivos Tasting
Room & Wine Shop
Grand Ave.
CARINA CELLARS
Wine Country
RUSACK
BECKMEN
BRANDER
BRIDLEWOOD
Ballard Canyon Rd.
Alamo Pintado
Baseline Rd.
Roblar Ave
Ballard Inn
LINCOURT
BLACKJACK RANCH
San Marcos Pass
BUTTONWOOD FARMS
RIDEAU

SOLVANG

Old Mission Wine Co.
Atterdang Rd.
Mission Dr.
Tastes of the Valleys
4th St.
PRESIDIO
LUCAS & LEWELLEN
Copenhagen Dr.
STOLPMAN
MANDOLINA
Oak St.
2nd St.
1st St.
Alisol Rd.

(*Photo above courtesy Jan Wolfinger*)

ADDAMO VINEYARDS

Guests entering Addamo Vineyards in Old Town Orcutt immediately realize they've discovered a different kind of tasting room. Owner David Addamo and his wife, Liz, have created an especially inviting atmosphere where visitors can relax and order delicious gourmet appetizers to complement the wines they sample. Every six weeks the tasting room hosts winemaker dinners prepared by Liz, a former restaurant owner and a graduate of the Le Cordon Bleu culinary institute in San Francisco. Named 2006's "Best Tasting Room" by the *Santa Maria Sun*, the Addamo tasting room sells wine by the glass and its extensive gift shop features wine accessories, logo ware, packaged gourmet food items, and custom-made wine baskets.

Addamo Vineyards was founded in 2000 with the planting of a 120-acre estate vineyard in the hills of northern Santa Barbara County. Seventy acres were planted to Pinot Noir, Addamo's principal varietal. In 2005, Addamo released its first vintages, which garnered four of the six medals awarded at the Santa Barbara County Fair Wine Competition.

"Our estate vineyard is just off the coast and benefits from the ocean breezes," explains David, who has an extensive agricultural background and hails from a family of farmers. "The sandy-loam soils and choice climate provide optimum conditions for growing exceptional fruit."

David and his staff regularly analyze the chemical components of the soil to ensure the growth of a low-yield crop—about one cluster per shoot.

"The chemistry starts in the soil," says David. "If you don't have quality soil you won't have quality wine."

At David's state-of-the-art production facility, only the finest German stainless-steel tanks and French oak barrels are used to make Addamo's award-winning vintages, which are allocated first to wine club members and to approximately 75 premier restaurants in Santa Barbara, Los Angeles, San Luis Obispo, and Monterey counties.

In fall 2008, Addamo will open a second, larger tasting room—a 38,000-square-foot Tuscan-style events center adjacent to the estate vineyard. The new venue will include a tasting room, banquet area, deli, gift shop, crush pad, and wine caves.

Addamo Vineyards
400 East Clark Avenue
Santa Maria, CA 93455
Opening fall 2008:
2510 East Clark Avenue
Santa Maria, CA 93455
(805) 937-6400
info@addamovineyards.com
www.addamovineyards.com

Sub-AVA: Santa Maria Valley

Owner: David Addamo

Tasting Hours:
11 a.m. – 7 p.m. Tuesday – Sunday

Wines: White Riesling, Chardonnay, Grenache, Dolcetto, Syrah, Pinot Noir, non-blended French and Italian varietals

Winemaker's Specialty: Pinot Noir

Winemaker: Justin Mund

Mixed Greens with Addamo Syrah Vinaigrette

2 Tbsp. balsamic vinegar
1 Tbsp. red-wine vinegar
1 Tbsp. Dijon mustard
1 tsp. light-brown sugar
1 clove garlic, crushed
1/2 tsp. salt
1/4 c. Addamo Syrah or sweet, berry-like red wine
1/4 tsp. ground pepper
3/4 c. olive oil
8 c. mixed greens

1/4 c. candied walnuts
1/4 medium red onion, sliced
1/4 c. blue cheese, crumbled
2 pears, sliced

Whisk first nine ingredients together, gradually adding oil. Toss with greens, walnuts, onion, and cheese. Place on individual serving plates and top with pear slices. Serve with **Addamo Syrah**.

ALEXANDER & WAYNE

Alexander & Wayne in Los Olivos is next door to the Arthur Earl Winery—both wineries are owned by Arthur "Art" White and Earl Brockelsby. Alexander & Wayne was founded first, in 1992, when the two friends and computer industry co-workers decided to change careers and become vintners.

At Alexander & Wayne, Art and Earl produce a wide variety of wines, from traditional California varietals—including those found in the Burgundy and Bordeaux regions of France—to an array of dessert wines. Most of the varietals are single-vineyard wines made from grapes purchased from select local growers with whom Alexander & Wayne has had long-standing contracts.

Art is the winemaker and likes what he calls "fruit-forward, full-bodied red wines and fresh, easy-drinking whites." He takes the minimalist approach to winemaking, letting the individual character of the grapes determine taste:

"My job is to find and purchase excellent fruit, then let the natural flavor come through," Art explains. "In the winery, I avoid doing anything that detracts from what nature and our growers have produced."

Using his "natural," hands-off technique, Art estimates that he "intervenes" in the winemaking process "no more than 10 percent of the time, to ensure consistency. Ninety percent of what's in the bottle is a reflection of what came from the vineyard."

Art and Earl are proud that Alexander & Wayne sells 98 percent of its wine directly to the consumer, through their tasting room and wine club. The two friends' approach to merchandizing their vintages mirrors Art's unadorned, common-sense style of making wine: "We want our customers to buy our wine because they tasted it and liked it," the partners agree, "not because they read a review or heard how good it was."

For that reason, Alexander & Wayne wines have never been entered in competitions or rated by wine critics. Alexander & Wayne wine is served in several local restaurants—the proprietors tasted Art and Earl's wine, liked it, and made arrangements to feature Alexander & Wayne on their wine lists.

Alexander & Wayne
2922 Grand Avenue
Los Olivos, CA 93441
(805) 688-9665
(800) 824-8584 toll free
info@alexanderandwayne.com
www.alexanderandwayne.com

Appellation of Origin:
Santa Barbara County

Owners:
Arthur White, Earl Brockelsby

Tasting Hours:
11 a.m. – 6 p.m. daily

Wines: Sauvignon Blanc, Chardonnay, Riesling, Pinot Noir, Merlot, Cabernet Franc, Cabernet Sauvignon, Bordeaux blends, Tempranillo, port

Winemaker's Specialty:
Pinot Noir

Winemaker: Arthur White

Caramelized Bananas and Vanilla Cream in Phyllo Cups

9 phyllo pastry sheets
1/2 c. (1 stick) butter, melted
8 Tbsp. sugar
1/2 c. sugar and sugar for topping
3-1/2 Tbsp. cornstarch
2 c. whole milk
4 large egg yolks
1/2 vanilla bean, split lengthwise, seeds removed
3 large, firm, ripe bananas, peeled and thinly sliced on diagonal
Chocolate sorbet

Stack pastry sheets and cut in half crosswise to form 18 8-1/2-inch by 13-inch rectangles. Butter every other cup in a 12-cup muffin pan. Brush one pastry piece with melted butter, sprinkle with 1/2 tsp. sugar. (Keep remaining pastry from drying out by covering with a damp towel.) Place another pastry piece on top of first, brush with butter, sprinkle with sugar; top with a third piece, brush with butter. Repeat process until you have 6 pastry stacks of three pieces each. Using a sharp knife and a 6-inch plate as a guide, cut out 6 6-inch-round stacks. Press each stack into one buttered muffin cup. Bake at 350° until golden, about 15 minutes. Remove cups and cool.

Whisk 1/2 cup sugar and cornstarch in a heavy saucepan. Gradually whisk in milk, then yolks. Add vanilla bean. Cook over medium heat, whisking continually, until cream thickens and boils, about 6 minutes. Strain cream into a small bowl, press plastic wrap directly onto surface. Chill 3 hours. Place phyllo cups on a baking sheet, spoon 1/3 cup cream into each cup, top with 5 or 6 banana slices. Sprinkle bananas with sugar. Broil until sugar caramelizes, about 2 minutes. Serve with chocolate sorbet and **Alexander & Wayne port.**

ALMA ROSA WINERY & VINEYARDS

Geographer Richard Sanford became a pioneering vintner and began an evolving winemaking adventure in 1971, when he planted Santa Barbara County's first Pinot Noir vines and co-founded the Sanford & Benedict Vineyard on Santa Rosa Road in the Santa Rita Hills. Ten years later, Richard and his wife, Thekla, left Sanford & Benedict to establish Sanford Winery & Vineyards, which for the next 25 years produced award-winning wines sold in 50 states and 16 countries.

In 2005, Richard and Thekla started in a new direction, leaving Sanford to found Alma Rosa Winery & Vineyards, with the goal of creating a benchmark standard of organic farming, sustainable agriculture, and environment-friendly commerce.

They named their new enterprise Alma Rosa—in Spanish, *alma* means "soul"— to express the soulful connection they enjoy with one another, their employees, and their Santa Rosa Road land, where they first became wine growers more than 30 years ago.

Alma Rosa's two vineyards are located in Santa Barbara County's coolest region, approximately 24 miles from the Pacific Ocean. "We have just the right climate to preserve the high acid and fruit flavor of the grapes," says Richard.

The La Encantada Vineyard (*encantada* means "enchanted") was planted in 2000 with Pinot Gris, Pinot Blanc, and seven clones of Pinot Noir. The El Jabali Vineyard (*jabalí* means "wild boar"), a small vineyard located a few miles east of La Encantada and established in 1983 as part of the Sanford Winery, is planted with Pinot Noir and Chardonnay.

Alma Rosa employs only sustainable farming practices, which include hand hoeing, the planting of cover crops for weed abatement, and the use of beneficial insects and sticky tape for insect control. No herbicides or pesticides are used. Both La Encantada and El Jabali receive yearly certification by the California Certified Organic Farmers and the USDA as 100-percent organic vineyards.

In keeping with Richard and Thekla's desire to operate an ecologically aware business, Alma Rosa wine is sold in returnable bottles that are sterilized and reused, and the couple's two vineyards provide refuge for endangered birds and other wildlife.

Alma Rosa Winery & Vineyards
7250 Santa Rosa Road
Buellton, CA 93427
(805) 688-9090
info@almarosawinery.com
www.almarosawinery.com

Sub-AVA: Santa Rita Hills

Owners:
Richard and Thekla Sanford

Tasting Hours:
11 a.m. – 4 p.m. daily

Wines: Pinot Gris, Pinot Blanc, Chardonnay, Pinot Noir, Pinot Noir-Vin Gris

Winemaker's Specialty: Pinot Noir

Winemaker: Christian Roguenant

Thai Chicken Soup

4 chicken breasts, grilled or roasted,
  skinned and cubed
4 14-oz. cans coconut milk
3 qts. chicken stock
4 bunches green onion, coarsely chopped
1/2 c. fresh ginger, chopped
1 bunch cilantro, leaves removed from stems
2 jalapeño chilies, seeded and chopped

1 Tbsp. curry powder
2 stalks lemongrass, chopped
Salt and pepper to taste
Sliced green onions for garnish
Whole cilantro leaves for garnish

Mix coconut milk, stock, onions, ginger, cilantro, chilies, curry, and lemongrass in a large stockpot and bring to a boil. Simmer for 5 minutes. Strain and season with salt and pepper. Ladle into individual bowls. Add chicken and garnish with cilantro leaves and chopped green onion. Serve with **Alma Rosa Pinot Gris**.
Recipe courtesy Catering Chef Gonzalo Pacheco, Wine Cask, Los Olivos

ARTHUR EARL WINERY

"Variety is our passion," says Arthur "Art" White, who with partner Earl Brockelsby founded Arthur Earl Winery in 1996 (Art and Earl also own Alexander & Wayne, established in 1992, but the two wineries are separately bonded). "We started Arthur Earl," explains Art, "because we wanted to make more varietals than one winery could handle."

All Arthur Earl wines are made in their Buellton winery, where they also produce wine for growers, wholesalers, and other wineries. Arthur Earl wines are made from grapes grown in Santa Barbara County, except for the Mourvèdre and Zinfandel, whose fruit comes from the warmer Paso Robles AVA. Art is the winemaker and produces very small quantities of Rhône and Northern Italian varietals as well as a California Zinfandel.

"Zinfandel is genetically the same as Primitivo, the Italian grape," Art points out. "Despite its origin, Zinfandel is probably the most 'Californian' of any variety grown in the state. My red wines are big, full-bodied, and fruit forward, while my whites are fresh, with a lot of flavor, and easy to drink."

Pinot Grigio, Nebbiolo, Barbera, and a red-wine blend named "Il Re"—"The King" in Italian—comprise Arthur Earl's Italian varietals. Rhône varietals include Viognier, Syrah, Mourvèdre, Grenache, Cinsaut, Counoise, as well as a special red-wine blend called "A Genoux," which in French means "to your knees"—the phrase comes from Alexander Dumas, author of *The Three Musketeers* and *The Count of Monte Christo*. The writer of swashbuckling adventures is said to have described his favorite wine as "so good that you should drink it on your knees with your hat off."

Art and Earl invite wine aficionados to visit their Los Olivos tasting room to experience the taste of Italy, France, and classic California—with their hats on or off.

Arthur Earl Winery
2922 Grand Avenue
P. O. Box 636
Los Olivos, CA 93441
(805) 693-1771
info@arthurearl.com
www.arthurearl.com

Appellation of Origin:
Santa Barbara County

Owners:
Arthur White, Earl Brockelsby

Tasting Hours:
11 a.m. – 6 p.m. daily

Wines: Viognier, Pinot Grigio, Syrah, Nebbiolo, Grenache, Mourvèdre, Barbera, Zinfandel, Moscato, Rhône blends

Winemaker's Specialties:
Syrah, Nebbiolo

Winemaker: Arthur White

Red Pepper Flan

2 to 3 large red bell peppers, stems removed
2 Tbsp. unsalted butter
2 Tbsp. all-purpose flour
2/3 c. milk
3 large eggs, beaten
6 Tbsp. Parmigiano-Reggiano cheese, grated
Large pinch each salt, freshly ground pepper, nutmeg

Bake peppers on a baking sheet at 375° for 30 to 45 minutes until soft. Cool, remove seeds and peel, and place in a colander and drain for 1 hour. Puree peppers until smooth, about 2 to 3 minutes. Melt butter in a medium-size saucepan. Whisk in flour and cook, whisking for 3 minutes. Add milk, whisking until smooth. Remove from heat, whisk in pepper puree, eggs, and remaining ingredients. Pour pepper mixture into 6 generously buttered 4-ounce molds and set in a baking dish; pour water two thirds of the way up the molds. Bake uncovered at 375° until flan puffs and is firm to the touch, about 30 minutes.

Run a knife around the inside of each mold and place a small serving plate on top, and invert to unmold. Serve with **Arthur Earl Barbera**.

ARTISTE WINERY & TASTING STUDIO

Artiste Winery & Tasting Studio is one of the most unusual and creatively decorated tasting rooms in Santa Barbara County. Located in the historic town of Santa Ynez, Artiste's tasting studio is designed as a 19th-century French Impressionist art studio equipped with painting easels for guests, who are invited to celebrate winemaking as an artistic expression.

Artiste is the brainchild of owner Bion Rice, who blends multiple wines or varietals made by other wineries to create cuvées ("cuvée" is a French term for a blend or special batch of wine).

Bion became interested in winemaking after attending college, when he marketed wine for his family's Santa Ynez winery, Sunstone Vineyards & Winery.

"The more time I spent in sales talking with sommeliers and consumers, the more I craved a deeper understanding of the craft of winemaking," says Bion. "I found that blending wines really appealed to my senses and for me was more creative. Each individual part of our cuvées is blended with the others to create a final, seamless wine that is much more than the sum of its parts. Artiste Winery was born from a desire to make world-class wine without concern for the typical classifications that tend to limit a winemaker's creativity."

Artiste wines are made only once and in very limited quanties. "Each wine is created as a tribute to the Old World wine producers, who have been blending wines for hundreds of years," explains Bion. "I use a bottle instead of a palette to create Impressionist-style wine blends, and hope that Artiste will open people's minds about blends and help them trust and share their own impressions."

The labels of all Artiste wines are reproductions of original paintings by international Impressionist-style artists, whose work is displayed on the tasting studio's walls. Artiste presents educational seminars on wine blending and cheese-and-wine pairing, hosts special events featuring guest chefs, and offers art classes in the adjoining art studio.

Artiste Winery & Tasting Studio
3569 Sagunto Street, Studio 102
P. O. Box 1320
Santa Ynez, CA 93460
(805) 686-2626
info@artiste.com
www.artiste.com

Appellation of Origin: California

Owner: Bion Rice

Tasting Hours:
11 a.m. – 5 p.m. daily

Wines: Red and white blends

Winemaker: Bion Rice

Grilled Australian Rack of Lamb with Potato-Artichoke Hash and Demi-Glaze

4 10- to 12-oz. racks of lamb, fat trimmed
5 Tbsp. canola oil, divided
4 medium shallots, chopped
1 Tbsp. plus 1 tsp. garlic, finely chopped, divided
2 c. Cabernet Sauvignon or Syrah wine
2 c. each chicken and beef stock
1 star anise, whole
Salt and pepper to taste
2 c. Yukon gold potatoes, diced
1 c. sweet potatoes, diced
2 c. fresh artichoke hearts, diced
1 c. red bell pepper, diced
2 bunches arugula leaves

1 c. yellow onion, diced
1 Tbsp. ginger, finely chopped

Demi-Glaze
Sauté shallots and 1 tsp. garlic in 2 Tbsp. oil over medium heat. Add wine and de-glaze pan. Simmer sauce until reduced by two thirds. Add stock and anise. Continue cooking until sauce coats the back of a spoon. Add salt and pepper, strain, and set aside.

Potato-Artichoke Hash
Blanch potatoes in salted water and set aside. Sauté artichoke hearts in 3 Tbsp. canola oil for 10 to 12 minutes,

stirring frequently. Add garlic, ginger, and bell pepper, and sauté until garlic is browned. Add potatoes and salt and pepper and sauté until potatoes are cooked and beginning to brown. Add arugula and cook until just wilted.

Rack of Lamb
Place racks of lamb on hot grill bone side down. Grill 6 minutes, turn, and grill 4 minutes. Let rest 2 minutes. Serve lamb and hash topped with demi-glaze with **Artiste "After Work"** Syrah or **"Perfecto"** cuvée.
Recipe courtesy Chef Budi Kazali, Café Chardonnay, The Ballard Inn

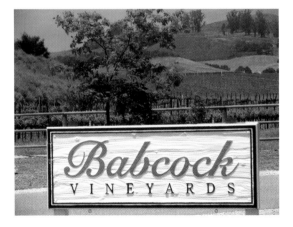

BABCOCK WINERY & VINEYARDS

In the late 1970s, Walt and Mona Babcock were searching for a peaceful retreat, a place to relax from the weekly demands of Walt's busy dental practice and the hectic schedule of operating two restaurants—the Babcocks' own Walt's Wharf in Seal Beach and Oyster's in Corona del Mar.

In 1978, Walt and Mona purchased 110 acres in the western Santa Ynez Valley, in the then-fledgling wine region that today is part of the Santa Rita Hills sub-AVA. Inspired by the area's emerging wine industry, Walt and Mona planted a 25-acre estate vineyard in 1980, with the intention of selling their fruit to local wineries.

"It was soon very apparent that the soil and cool climate of our estate was ideal for producing ultra-premium wine grapes," says Walt.

The Babcocks realized that the fruit they were selling their customers was producing award-winning wines, and in 1984 they began making their own wine under the Babcock Vineyards label.

As Walt and Mona were deciding to start the winery, their son, Bryan—an Occidental College graduate with a major in biology and a minor in chemistry—was attending the University of California, Davis, working toward a master's degree in food science with an emphasis in enology. It was only natural that Bryan became the Babcock winemaker—one of his first wines, a 1984 Estate Sauvignon Blanc, won a double-gold medal.

Today, the Babcock estate vineyard comprises 80 acres and Bryan is lauded as an accomplished winemaker. The *Los Angeles Times* has chosen him as one of the "Ten Best Winemakers of the Year," and as the "Most Courageous Winemaker of the Year" for "his daring winemaking style."

Bryan describes his style as "integrative."

"I analyze the fundamental elements I have to work with—microclimates, soil types, canopy management, and irrigation—to understand the potential for producing the wine I want to make," Bryan explains. "Then I integrate those materials to create a quality wine at a reasonable price."

Babcock Winery & Vineyards
5175 East Highway 246
Lompoc, CA 93436
P. O. Box 637
Lompoc, CA 93438-0637
(805) 736-1455
info@babcockwinery.com
www.babcockwinery.com

Sub-AVA: Santa Rita Hills

Owners: The Babcock family

Tasting Hours:
10:30 a.m. – 4 p.m. daily

Wines: Chardonnay, Sauvignon Blanc, Pinot Gris, Pinot Noir, Cabernet Sauvignon, Syrah

Winemaker: Bryan Babcock

Coconut, Lemongrass, and Leek Broth with King Prawns

36 king prawns, cooked and diced
4 14-oz. cans coconut milk
3 qts. chicken stock
2 stalks leeks, coarsely chopped
1/2 c. ginger, chopped
1 bunch cilantro
2 jalapeño chilies, seeded and chopped
1 Tbsp. curry powder
2 stalks lemongrass, chopped
Curry-infused olive oil for garnish

Sliced leeks for garnish
Whole cilantro leaves for garnish

Mix coconut milk, stock, leeks, ginger, cilantro, chilies, curry, and lemongrass in a large stockpot and bring to a boil. Simmer for 5 minutes. Strain and season with salt and pepper. Ladle into individual bowls. Add prawns and garnish with curry-infused olive oil, cilantro leaves, and sliced leeks. Serve with **Babcock Chardonnay**.
Recipe courtesy Chef Jeremy Tummel, Wine Cask, Santa Barbara

BECKMEN VINEYARDS

Before Tom Beckmen became a vintner, he had a prosperous career in the music industry as the founder of the Los Angeles-based Roland Corporation U. S., a synthesizer and electronic keyboard manufacturer. Tom credits much of his business success to his ability to "continually evolve and test myself and embrace new challenges." When Tom sold the Roland Corporation in 1993, he already had plans for his new venture—wine growing.

Tom's father was a cattle buyer in the Santa Ynez Valley and as a boy Tom worked on a local ranch. In 1994, Tom returned to the valley, purchasing a neglected 40-acre parcel with an existing winery on Ontiveros Road. Tom says that he and his son, Steve, began "polishing this jewel in the rough, completely replanting the property while introducing modern viticulture techniques."

Steve was Tom's "ideal choice" for winemaker—Tom appreciated Steve's studies in archeology at the University of California, Santa Cruz, his love for agriculture, and Steve's "skill in analytical thinking." A self-taught winemaker, Steve honed his craft by working closely with several Santa Barbara viticulturists. He also traveled to wine-growing regions around the world to study both classic and the latest winemaking techniques and to learn what he calls "viticulture's trade secrets."

For two years, Tom and Steve successfully crafted small lots of Cabernet Sauvignon and Sauvignon Blanc at their newly established winery. In 1996, father and son were "awed and inspired" by a 365-acre hillside property they purchased in Ballard Canyon, three miles from the winery. The Beckmens named their new holding Purisima Mountain Vineyard, in admiration for the location's wine-growing attributes.

"The property's 1,250-foot elevation, microclimate, and limestone soils make it a winemaker's treasure," says Tom. "It contains all the necessary elements to produce world-class Rhône varietals."

Today, Beckmen Vineyards produces a full line of Rhône-style wines. Tom and Steve are proud of their accomplishment: "We believe we've achieved a rare dream, building a winery and a philosophy of viticulture from the ground up."

Beckmen Vineyards
2670 Ontiveros Road
P. O. Box 542
Los Olivos, CA 93441
(805) 688-8664
info@beckmenvineyards.com
www.beckmenvineyards.com

Sub-AVA: Santa Ynez Valley

Owners:
Tom Beckmen, Steve Beckmen

Tasting Hours:
11 a.m. – 5 p.m. daily

Wines: Syrah, Grenache, Grenache Rosé, Marsanne, Cabernet Sauvignon, Sauvignon Blanc, Rhône varietals and blends

Winemaker's Specialties:
Syrah, Grenache

Winemaker: Steve Beckmen

Wild-Mushroom Risotto Cakes

1-1/2 lbs. wild mushrooms, cut into bite-size pieces
1/2 c. peanut oil
1 medium onion, minced
2 large shallots, minced
1 large garlic clove, minced
2 c. arborio rice
1-1/2 c. Beckmen Vineyards Le Bec Blanc
7 c. mushroom and/or vegetable stock, heated
3 Tbsp. olive oil
Salt and pepper
2 medium tomatoes, peeled, seeded, and chopped

6 Tbsp. unsalted butter, chilled, cut into small pieces
1/2 c. Parmesan, grated
Large pinch chopped Italian parsley
Freshly ground pepper
1/2 c. canola oil

Sauté onion, shallots, and garlic 3 to 4 minutes. Add rice and stir. Add wine to deglaze pan and cook, stirring often, until liquid is absorbed. Add 3 cups stock and cook, stirring often, until liquid is absorbed. Add 3 cups stock, a large pinch of salt, and tomatoes, and turn flame to high. Cook and stir until almost al dente. Sauté mushrooms in olive oil 3 to 4

minutes. Add mushrooms and 1 cup stock to risotto. Remove from flame, and vigorously beat in butter and Parmesan until dissolved. Stir in parsley and salt and pepper to taste.

Pour risotto onto a greased baking sheet. Cover and chill overnight. Cut risotto into cakes with a cookie cutter. Sauté in canola oil 1 minute on each side. Bake cakes for 5 minutes at 375°. Top with Parmesan and parsley and serve with **Beckmen Estate Grenache**.
Recipe courtesy Brett Larson

BEDFORD THOMPSON WINERY & VINEYARD

Since 1993, Bedford Thompson Winery & Vineyard has made handcrafted single-variety wines from grapes grown in the hills of the Los Alamos Valley.

"The area is particularly well suited for Rhône varieties," says owner and winemaker Stephen Bedford.

The critics seem to agree. *The Wine Advocate*'s Robert Parker writes, "It's hard to find a better Cabernet Franc from Southern California than Bedford Thompson's." And the *Los Angeles Times* describes Bedford Thompson wines as "marvelously crafted . . . a beautiful basis at a great price."

Stephen is a winemaking veteran. In the late 1970s, he earned a degree in food science from the University of California, Los Angeles, and worked for an agricultural research lab before joining a Cupertino winery. In 1982, he became the winemaker at Mt. Eden Vineyards in Saratoga. Three years later, Stephen moved to the cool-climate region of northern Santa Barbara County, where he became winemaker at Rancho Sisquoc Winery and began consulting for local wineries.

"The cool-climate experience I had at the Northern California wineries primed me for the transition to Santa Barbara County," says Stephen.

Stephen began an independent winemaking operation in 1993, co-founding Bedford Thompson Winery & Vineyard. He produced the winery's first vintage in 1994 and became the sole proprietor in July 2003.

The Bedford Thompson vineyards are planted on steep, south-facing hills along Alisos Canyon Road. "The steep terrain creates optimum conditions to grow fruit with wonderfully complex and deeply concentrated flavors," explains Stephen. "Bedford Thompson is well known for rich, inky Syrah, Grenache, Petite Sirah, and Mourvèdre."

White grapes are pressed as whole clusters and fermented in barrels, while red grapes are fermented in small, open-top tanks and punched down.

"This process ensures balance and complexity in the whites and maximum extraction and flavor in the reds," says Stephen. "All of my wines have a moderate alcohol content so they have longevity and balance and pair well with food."

Bedford Thompson Winery & Vineyard
448 Bell Street
P. O. Box 507
Los Alamos, CA 93440
(805) 344-2107
tastingroom@bedfordthompson
  winery.com
www.bedfordthompsonwinery.com

Appellation of Origin:
Santa Barbara County

Owner: Stephen Bedford

Tasting Hours:
1 a.m. – 5 p.m. daily

Wines: Chardonnay, Pinot Grigio, Gewürztraminer, Cabernet Franc, Syrah, Grenache, Mourvèdre

Winemaker: Stephen Bedford

French Beefsteak with Potatoes and Sauce Maitre d'Hotel

2 lbs. beef filets, cut into 6 pieces
1/2 c. olive oil
1/2 tsp. salt
12 medium white rose potatoes, peeled and
  cut lengthwise into pieces
4 sticks unsalted butter
1/2 c. parsley
Juice of one lemon
Salt and pepper to taste

Mix olive oil and salt in a bowl, pour over filets in a zip-lock bag and marinate 2 hours. Broil or grill filets over high heat, about 5 minutes per side. While meat is cooking, boil butter in a saucepan until milk solids have separated to the bottom. Ladle out 1 cup of the clarified butter and heat 1/2 cup in a medium skillet. Fry potatoes in the hot butter, turning until cooked through and browned. Remove from skillet and keep warm. Bring 1 cup water to a boil in a saucepan, add parsley, and boil 3 minutes. Remove parsley, place in cold water 5 minutes, then strain and chop. Pour remaining 1/2 cup clarified butter into a saucepan and add parsley, lemon juice, salt, and pepper. Beat hard with a whisk and bring to a boil. Remove from heat. Place filets on a platter with potatoes and pour sauce over all. Serve with **Bedford Thompson Mourvèdre**.

BLACKJACK RANCH VINEYARDS & WINERY

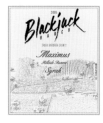

When Blackjack Ranch Vineyards & Winery owner Roger Wisted was 14 years old, he began studying the wines and winemaking techniques of California and France. Two years later, he was fermenting wine in the produce section of his parents' grocery store, and by age 17 he was collecting wines from the Bordeaux and Burgundy regions of France.

But it was Roger's entrepreneurial creativity in the world of gaming that allowed him to pursue his dream of planting a vineyard and building a winery.

Blackjack Ranch is named after a new version of the card game "21"—Roger invented, patented, copyrighted, and trademarked "California Blackjack" in 1990. Roger's game is played to 22 points instead of 21, and players bet against each other, not the house. Considered a game different from "21," California Blackjack is legally licensed to card clubs and casinos throughout the state. (An 1873 California anti-gambling law still on the books forbids the playing of "21"—a stricture that does not affect gaming at Native-American casinos.)

In 1996, Roger used the copyright proceeds from California Blackjack to purchase property on Alamo Pintado Road in Solvang. The land is planted with Syrah, Merlot, Cabernet Franc, and Chardonnay, and varies from flat to steeply mountainous. Precipitous portions of the terrain inspired names for two of the vineyard blocks—Billy Goat and Suicide hills. Hamburger's Hill is named after a Black Angus cow that once shared the hill with Blackjack Ranch Vineyards.

In 1997, Blackjack produced its first two vintages, which were both awarded 90 points by world-renowned wine critic Robert Parker in *The Wine Advocate* magazine.

Roger constructed Blackjack's "California Rustic" tasting room in 1999 from materials salvaged from old buildings that once stood on the property. Wood from one of the lanes at the old Solvang Bowling Alley was used to construct the tasting bar. Roger's temperature-controlled wine cellar displays "Hall of Fame" wines, classic varietals from California and France dating back 60 years.

Blackjack Ranch Vineyards & Winery
2205 Alamo Pintado Road
Solvang, CA 93463
(805) 686-4492
roger@blackjackranch.com
www.blackjackranch.com

Sub-AVA: Santa Ynez Valley

Owner: Roger Wisted

Tasting Hours:
11 a.m. – 5 p.m. Thurs. – Mon.

Wines: Chardonnay, Pinot Noir, Merlot, Syrah, Cabernet Franc, Bordeaux blends

Winemaker's Specialty: "Harmonie" Bordeaux blend

Winemaker: Roger Wisted

Arugula-Prosciutto Appetizer Rolls

1 lb. prosciutto
1 bag large arugula leaves
4 to 6 oz. Gorgonzola cheese, room temperature
1/2 c. currants, soaked in hot water

Place one slice prosciutto on a flat surface. Place two arugula leaves, end to end, on top of one end of the prosciutto so the leaves extend over the edges of the ham. Spread 1/4 to 1/2 tsp. Gorgonzola over the arugula. Top with 4 to 5 currants. Starting at the end of the prosciutto slice with the filling, roll the ham and place seam side down on a serving platter. Repeat with remaining ingredients. Serve with **Blackjack Ranch Chardonnay.**

THE BRANDER VINEYARD & DOMAINE SANTA BARBARA

The Brander Vineyard's château-style tasting room, with its beamed ceilings, tiled floors, French doors, and rustic courtyard set among flowers and redwood, poplar, and cottonwood trees offers the ambience of a small European wine estate. The Argentine and Swedish flags that fly with the stars and stripes high above the tasting room add to the winery's international flavor while honoring the Brander family's heritage.

Fred Brander, a pioneer of the Santa Barbara County wine industry, creates world-class Sauvignon Blanc in a variety of styles, as well as small quantities of handcrafted Bordeaux-style red wines. A graduate in enology from the University of California, Davis, Fred founded the Brander Vineyard in 1975 to produce estate-bottled Sauvignon Blanc, which for many years was the winery's only varietal. His extensive experimentation with Sauvignon Blanc has earned him a reputation as one of California's winemaking experts.

Today the Brander Vineyard bottles seven distinctly different Sauvignon Blancs. Fred makes his wines in true French fashion, with high levels of acid to ensure age worthiness. Brander's "Au Natural" is Sauvignon Blanc in its purest form, in the style of the wines of the Loire Valley in Southern France. In keeping with the French tradition of naming a cuvée (blend) after a winery owner's first-born child, two Brander Sauvignon Blanc cuvées are named after Fred's twins—"Cuvée Natalie" is created from varietals from France's Alsace region (bordering Germany) and "Cuvée Nicolas" is made from varietals of Bordeaux.

In 1995 Fred established Domaine Santa Barbara to produce premium Burgundian varietals. Domaine's focus is Chardonnay and vineyard-designated wines that highlight the diverse *terroir* of some of the best vineyards of the Santa Maria, Los Alamos, and Santa Ynez valleys.

The Brander Vineyard & Domaine Santa Barbara

2401 Refugio Road
P. O. Box 92
Los Olivos, CA 93441
(805) 688-2455
(800) 970-9979 toll free
info@brander.com
www.brander.com

Sub-AVA: Santa Ynez Valley

Owner: Fred Brander

Tasting Hours:
10 a.m. – 5 p.m. daily
(mid-April – mid-Oct.)
11 a.m. – 4 p.m. daily
(mid-Oct. – mid-April)

Wines: Sauvignon Blanc, red Bordeaux varietals

Winemaker's Specialties:
Seven styles of Sauvignon Blanc

Winemaker: Fred Brander

Classic Duck Cassoulet

1 5-lb. duck, trimmed of fat, pierced with fork, cut into 8 pieces
6 15-oz. cans white beans, drained, liquid reserved
8 oz. thick-sliced bacon, cut into 1-inch squares
3 carrots, thickly sliced
2 medium onions, coarsely chopped
5 cloves garlic, minced
1 28-oz. can diced tomatoes, drained, liquid reserved
1/4 tsp. dried thyme, crumbled
Salt and freshly ground pepper to taste
1-1/2 lbs. Kielbasa sausage, cooked and sliced
1/2 c. fresh bread crumbs

Heat beans in saucepan. Fry bacon in a large, heavy skillet, drain, and stir into beans. Brown duck in skillet over medium high heat, about 10 minutes, then drain on paper towels. Reserve duck fat. Add carrots and onions to skillet, cooking until soft. Add garlic, cooking 2 minutes, then tomatoes, cooking 3 minutes. Add 1 cup reserved bean liquid and scrape brown bits from pan. Return duck to skillet, sprinkle with thyme. Add bean liquid to partially cover duck. Cover and simmer until duck is tender, about 1-1/4 hours. Remove duck and spoon off fat; reserve.

Grease a large Dutch oven. Sprinkling each layer with salt and pepper, layer bean mixture, sausage, duck pieces, duck broth with vegetables, and bean mixture. Add more bean liquid if necessary to come to top of beans without covering them. Sprinkle with 1/4 cup bread crumbs and drizzle with 2 Tbsp. duck fat. Cover and bake 35 minutes at 325°. Remove cover, break crust into pieces with a spoon, and fold into cassoulet. Turn up oven to 400° and bake 45 minutes. Add reserved tomato liquid if cassoulet seems dry. Sprinkle with remaining bread crumbs and drizzle with 2 Tbsp. duck fat. Bake about 20 minutes longer, until top is crusty and golden. Serve with **Brander Cotes du Rhône.**

BRIDLEWOOD ESTATE WINERY

One of Santa Barbara County's most inviting wine-tasting destinations is the Bridlewood Estate Winery, where visitors can encounter the ambience of a California horse ranch. Bridlewood is a former equine rehabilitation center—about a dozen horses are still stabled near the lake beyond the tasting room. The ranch became a winery in 1998 when 40 of its 150 acres were planted with Rhône varietals.

Bridlewood Estate makes a variety of wines, including seven blends of Syrah, its flagship wine, as well as small lots of "flavor-profile Syrah." Winemaker David Hopkins is specific and descriptive in detailing the Syrah wines he crafts:

"Central Coast Syrah is blended from grapes grown in various microclimates throughout the Central Coast to create a layered, complex wine. By sourcing fruit from distinctive vineyards, I can work with multiple flavors, aromas, and textures to deliver a specific flavor profile. These wines showcase the range of styles that can be made from Syrah and they are sold exclusively through the wine club and in our tasting room."

Bridlewood's enormous mission-style tasting room features a red-tile roof with a bell tower and a richly paneled tasting bar, where the winery displays its many awards. On cold days, guests can sample Bridlewood's current offerings while warming themselves at the fireplace, and in every weather visitors can browse the extensive gift shop that sells wine accessories, art, and logo t-shirts and caps.

The winery's setting is exquisitely landscaped with manicured lawns and hedges, abundant roses, and trees that line the driveway. A gazebo stands beside a life-size metal sculpture of a horse, a tribute to the equines that once came to the ranch to rest and heal.

Guests are welcome to bring a picnic lunch and to spend the day relaxing and strolling the grounds. Camera buffs are encouraged to take advantage of Bridlewood's panorama of vineyards and gardens and their changing seasonal colors.

Bridlewood Estate Winery
3555 Roblar Avenue
Santa Ynez, CA 93460
(805) 688-9000
(800) 467-4100 toll free
info@bridlewoodwinery.com
www.bridlewoodwinery.com

Sub-AVA: Santa Ynez Valley

Owner: E. J. Gallo Winery

Tasting Hours:
10 a.m. – 5 p.m. daily

Wines: Viognier, Chardonnay, Sauvignon Blanc, Pinot Noir, Syrah, Cabernet Sauvignon, Zinfandel, Merlot, port

Winemaker's Specialty: Syrah

Winemaker: David Hopkins

Drunken Chicken

4 chicken breasts, skinned, boned, and cut in half
Salt and pepper to taste
1 c. flour
2 Tbsp. butter
2 Tbsp. olive oil
1 large onion, finely chopped
2 Tbsp. parsley, chopped
1 16-oz. can diced tomatoes with liquid
1/4 tsp. ground cloves
1/2 tsp. cinnamon
1 Tbsp. brown sugar
1/2 c. raisins
1 c. dry sherry or vermouth
1/2 c. slivered almonds

Season chicken with salt and pepper and dredge in flour. In a large skillet, melt butter and add oil. Brown chicken and place in a 3-quart baking dish. Add onions to the skillet and cook until transparent. Add parsley, tomatoes and liquid, cloves, cinnamon, sugar, raisins, and sherry or vermouth. Simmer uncovered for 15 to 20 minutes, stirring occasionally. Pour over chicken, sprinkle with almonds, and bake at 375° for 30 minutes. Serve with **Bridlewood Syrah**.

BUTTONWOOD FARM WINERY & VINEYARD

Buttonwood Farm Winery & Vineyard is named for the buttonwood tree, a species of sycamore native to Santa Barbara County. The buttonwood's name derives from its distinctive feature—the brown, button-like seed clusters that hang on long stems from the branches.

Louisiana native Betty Williams founded Buttonwood Farm in 1968, when she moved to Solvang from Southern California after her children were grown. Betty loved agriculture and horses and purchased the 106-acre property to plant an orchard and build a thoroughbred breeding facility.

Twenty years later, a vintner friend of Betty's tested the soil at Buttonwood Farm. He told her that the sun-drenched mesa on the eastern portion of the farm would be an ideal place for a vineyard. A longtime wine aficionado, Betty began a three-year planting process, choosing varietals that reflected her and son-in-law Bret Davenport's taste for Bordeaux and Rhône-style wines: Sauvignon Blanc, Semillon, Marsanne, Merlot, Cabernet Sauvignon, Cabernet Franc, and Syrah. In the following years, the vineyard increased in size to 39 acres.

In 1989, Betty and Bret constructed a winery, just in time for Buttonwood's first bottling. That same year, Australian winemaker Michael Brown joined the Buttonwood team. Michael, a graduate of the University of California, Davis, had honed his winemaking skills by working for six years at wineries in Santa Barbara County.

All Buttonwood vintages are made from grapes grown exclusively in its estate vineyards, which are cultivated in accordance with principles of sustainable farming. Michael explains that he makes wine "that is not only meant to be enjoyed with food but that also has great aging potential."

Buttonwood's colorful wine label is the work of Betty's daughter, artist Seyburn Zorthian. Seyburn's studies of abstract brush-stroke technique in Japan inspired her to create the design that suggests the image of a grapevine while retaining the dynamic mystery of non-representational art.

Buttonwood Farm Winery & Vineyard
1500 Alamo Pintado Road
Solvang, CA 93463
P. O. Box 1007
Solvang, CA 93464
(805) 688-3032
(800) 715-1404 toll free
info@buttonwoodwinery.com
www.buttonwoodwinery.com

Sub-AVA: Santa Ynez Valley

Owners: Bret Davenport, Seyburn Zorthian, Barry Zorthian

Tasting Hours:
11 a.m. – 5 p.m. daily

Wines: Sauvignon Blanc, Merlot, Cabernet Sauvignon, Cabernet Franc, Syrah, Marsanne

Winemaker's Specialty:
Sauvignon Blanc

Winemaker: Michael Brown

Buttonwood Crab Cakes

1 lb. crab
1/2 c. onion, chopped
1/2 c. each red and green bell peppers, chopped
2 eggs
3 Tbsp. Buttonwood Sauvignon Blanc
1 Tbsp. white Worcestershire sauce
1 Tbsp. lemon juice
1 Tbsp. grated lemon rind
1 Tbsp chopped basil
1 tsp. dry mustard
1/2 tsp. ground red pepper

2 c. seasoned bread crumbs
2 to 4 Tbsp. butter

Mix crab, vegetables, seasonings, and 1 cup bread crumbs in a bowl. Shape into patties and dredge in remaining bread crumbs. Melt butter in a skillet. Cook crab cakes over medium heat until golden brown on both sides. Serve with **Buttonwood Sauvignon Blanc**.

CAMBRIA ESTATE VINEYARDS & WINERY

Cambria Estate Vineyards & Winery is situated on a portion of the historic Rancho Tepusquet, an 1838 Spanish land grant. The Chumash Indians named the area "*tepuztli*," which means "copper coin," and later Spanish settlers pronounced the word "tepusquet." In the 19th century, the rancho supported cattle and row crops. In the early 1970s Tepusquet Vineyard was planted and the old Spanish ranchland became part of Santa Barbara County's burgeoning international wine scene.

Husband and wife Jess Jackson and Barbara Banke purchased 1,400 acres of the Tepusquet Vineyard in 1987 and renamed it "Cambria"—the Roman word for "Wales"— in honor of their family heritage.

"Tepusquet Vineyard had a reputation for site-specific, character-laden Chardonnay and Pinot Noir," explains Barbara, who manages the winemaking facility and supervises all vineyard operations. "We purchased the premium part of the vineyard to make great wines that capture the unmistakable flavor of the Santa Maria Bench."

The Santa Maria Bench—a "bench" is a raised, level tract of land—lies in the eastern Santa Maria Valley along the banks of the Sisquoc River, beside the foothills of the San Rafael Mountains. The bench's soil is a shallow, gravelly, exceptionally well-draining loam that restricts vine vigor and produces concentrated and intense varietal flavors.

Four distinct vineyards comprise Cambria Estate Vineyards & Winery: Tepusquet and Bench Break and "Katherine's" and "Julia's," which are named after Jess and Barbara's daughters. Barbara points out that the land's unusual mineral characteristics are most evident in the austerest area of the estate, the Bench Break Vineyard. Cambria's special soils are embodied in the grapes that make the wine—a fact that perfectly suits winemaker Denise Shurtleff, who believes varietal characteristics should be solidly developed before fruit is ever harvested:

"The lush, tropical notes of Chardonnay, the dense fruit concentration of Pinot Noir, and the rich spiciness of Syrah are captured only if developed in the vineyard," Denise says. "I barrel-ferment Cambria's Chardonnay and allow it to age *sur lie* to intensify palate feel and fruit bouquet. Pinot Noir and Syrah are cold soaked to heighten color and extract complex flavors."

Cambria Estate Vineyards & Winery
5475 Chardonnay Lane
Santa Maria, CA 93454
(805) 937-8091
info@cambriawines.com
www.cambriawines.com

Sub-AVA: Santa Maria Valley

Owner: Barbara Banke

Tasting Hours:
10 a.m. – 5 p.m. daily

Wines: Chardonnay, Pinot Noir, Syrah, Viognier, Sangiovese, Pinot Gris

Winemaker's Specialties: Chardonnay, Pinot Noir, Syrah

Winemaker: Denise Shurtleff

Wild Mushroom and Goat Cheese Bruschetta

2 oz. oyster mushrooms, coarsely chopped
4 oz. shitake mushrooms, coarsely chopped
5 oz. portobello mushrooms, coarsely chopped
2 Tbsp. olive oil
1 Tbsp. unsalted butter
2 large garlic cloves, minced
1 shallot, minced
1/4 c. dry sherry

1/4 c. chicken stock
1 tsp. dried thyme
1/2 tsp. dried basil
Kosher salt and red pepper flakes to taste
1 French-bread baguette, sliced into 16 thin slices
3 to 4 oz. fresh goat cheese, room temperature
Lemon zest
Fresh chives, snipped

In a large sauté pan or skillet, heat olive oil and butter over medium heat. Add garlic and shallot and sauté for 1 to 2 minutes, stirring frequently. Raise heat slightly and add mushrooms. Sauté for 7 to 8 minutes. Add sherry, chicken stock, thyme, and basil and cook until liquid is evaporated. Season with salt and pepper. Keep warm. Preheat broiler. Spread baguette slices first with goat cheese and then with mushroom mixture. Place on a broiler pan. Broil for 3 to 4 minutes or until mushrooms just begin to brown on top. Remove from oven and place on serving dish. Garnish with lemon zest and chives. Serve with **Cambria Julia's Vineyard Pinot Noir**.

CARINA CELLARS

What happens when an avid wine collector with a dream meets an accomplished winemaker with a vision?

Welcome to Carina Cellars, founded by attorney and businessman David Hardee and winemaker Joey Tensley. The partners have received rave reviews from Santa Barbara County wine critics, including the *Santa Barbara News-Press'* Dennis Schaefer, who wrote, "In my mind, this is a 'can't miss' proposition and the proof is in the bottle."

Joey began his career in 1993, working for several successful local wineries, including Fess Parker, Babcock, and Beckmen. In 2002, he began making wine under his own label, Tensley Wine Company. That same year Joey met David. The two discussed their mutual ambition to establish a winery and agreed that David's business acumen combined with Joey's viticulture skills would create an ideal partnership. "Joey and I teamed up to make wines that emphasize the Santa Barbara County *terroir*," explains David.

Carina Cellars purchases grapes from growers that share David and Joey's philosophy of farming. "Our growers have a dedication to canopy management, low yields, and vine balance," says David. "Once we receive the fruit at the winery, we take a traditional and minimalist approach to winemaking to let those beautiful characteristics of the vineyards shine through."

The winery produces Rhône-style, vineyard-designated varietals and blends as well as Santa Barbara County Viognier, Syrah, Cabernet Sauvignon, Grenache, and Mourvèdre. David and Joey believe that tasting a wine is a personal experience that shouldn't be overshadowed by the wine's accolades, awards, or price. They want guests to taste the nuances of Carina Cellars wines and feel comfortable, whether they are first-time tasters or seasoned aficionados—Carina Cellars wines are not rated or entered in competitions, and their prices do not appear on the tasting room's wine list.

Visitors to the spacious and airy Carina Cellars tasting room may also sample offerings from Tensley Wine Company, as well as browse the gift shop, which features a variety of gourmet food items, pasta sauces, vinegars, oils, olives, wine accessories, and logo t-shirts and caps.

Carina Cellars
2900 Grand Avenue
P. O. Box 644
Los Olivos, CA 93441
(805) 688-2459
tastingroom@carinacellars.com
www.carinacellars.com

Sub-AVA: Santa Ynez Valley

Owner: David Hardee

Tasting Hours:
11 a.m. – 5 p.m. daily

Wines: Viognier, Syrah, Cabernet Sauvignon, Grenache, Mourvèdre, red wine blends

Winemaker's Specialties:
"Iconoclast," "7 % Syrah"

Winemaker: Joey Tensley

Risotto with Butternut Squash and Leeks

1 2-lb. butternut squash, peeled, seeded, and cut into 1/2-inch pieces
4 Tbsp. olive oil
Salt and pepper
6 c. vegetable stock
3 large leeks (white and pale-green parts only), thinly sliced (about 3 c.)
2 c. arborio rice or medium-grain white rice
1/2 c. dry white wine
1/2 c. Parmesan cheese, grated
2 Tbsp. fresh sage, chopped

Place squash on large rimmed baking sheet. Drizzle with 2 Tbsp. olive oil, sprinkle with salt and pepper, and toss to coat. Roast about 40 minutes at 400° until tender and slightly brown, stirring occasionally. Bring stock to a simmer in a heavy saucepan. Reduce heat to low, cover, and keep warm. Heat 2 Tbsp. oil over medium-low heat in another heavy large saucepan. Add leeks and sauté about 10 minutes until soft but not brown. Add rice; stir 1 minute. Add wine and simmer about 2 minutes until absorbed, stirring constantly. Add 1/2 cup hot stock; simmer until absorbed, stirring frequently. Add remaining stock 1/2 cup at a time, stirring frequently and allowing stock to be absorbed before adding more. Cook about 25 minutes, until rice is tender and mixture is creamy. Add roasted squash, Parmesan cheese, and sage; stir until heated through. Season to taste with salt and pepper. Serve with **Carina Cellars "Iconoclast."**

COLD HEAVEN CELLARS

Cold Heaven Cellars has created a successful and unrivaled niche in the Santa Barbara County winemaking community by specializing in Viognier. *Los Angeles Times* wine critic Patrick Comiskey finds Cold Heaven's Viognier "so rare and audacious that it just might be the first Viognier to shoulder its way into cult status."

Owner and winemaker Morgan Clendenen makes five Viogniers under two labels:

The Cold Heaven label specializes in four single-vineyard, cool-climate Viogniers made from grapes grown in Santa Barbara County.

And the Domaine des Deux Mondes label features "Deux C," an international, 50/50 blend—half the grapes come from France's Condrieu appellation in the northern Rhône Valley and are provided by Morgan's friend and legendary winemaker Yves Cuilleron, and half come from the Sanford & Benedict Vineyard in Santa Barbara County.

Morgan's career began when she worked for a North Carolina wine distributor, then as a sales rep for a Napa winery, where she learned the industry from the inside out, acquiring knowledge from Northern California's premier winemakers and grape growers: "Over time, I built upon that experience, which accounts for where I am today," she says.

In 1996, Morgan moved to Santa Barbara County and founded Cold Heaven Cellars with the intent of producing one varietal—Viognier. "I saw something I could really hang my hat on," she says, "a varietal I could define and pioneer in California, in a way that Viognier hadn't been done before."

Morgan regularly travels throughout California and Condrieu, tasting Viogniers to determine which clones grow best within different wine-growing areas. Her research into individual vineyards and their microclimates has helped her determine the proper time to harvest the fruit. "Viognier can be difficult to grow," Morgan explains. "If you harvest the grapes too late, the acids that provide structure will disappear. Viognier that maintains a natural acidity is the best expression of the grape."

Today, Cold Heaven also makes Pinot Noir and Syrah from the Clendenen family's Le Bon Climat Vineyard in the Santa Maria Valley, and specialty wines under the Clendenen Family Vineyards label from their estate plantings at Bien Nacido Vineyard.

Cold Heaven Cellars
448-B Bell Street
P. O. Box 42
Los Alamos, CA 93440
(805) 344-3640
info@coldheavencellars.com
www.coldheavencellars.com

Sub-AVA: Santa Rita Hills

Owner: Morgan Clendenen

Tasting Hours:
11 a.m. – 5 p.m. Friday – Sunday
And by appointment

Wines: Viognier, Pinot Noir, Syrah

Winemaker's Specialty: Viognier

Winemaker: Morgan Clendenen

Salad Niçoise

1-1/2 lbs. tuna steaks
8 c. sweet baby greens lettuce
1 lb. small rose potatoes, cooked and cooled
1/2 lb. green beans, trimmed, steamed, and cooled
3 tomatoes cut into wedges
3 hard-boiled eggs, quartered lengthwise
1/2 c. niçoise or black olives
2 Tbsp. capers
Salt and pepper to taste

Vinaigrette:
1/2 c. extra virgin olive oil
2 Tbsp. balsamic vinegar
1 Tbsp. each Dijon mustard and
    lemon juice
1 Tbsp. minced scallions or shallots
1 Tbsp. herbs de Provence
Salt and pepper to taste

Mix vinaigrette ingredients in a bowl or shaker jar. Brush tuna steaks with

a small amount of vinaigrette. Grill or broil tuna to desired doneness. Break into bite-size chunks. Divide lettuce equally and place on individual serving plates. Arrange tuna, potatoes, green beans, tomatoes, eggs, olives, and capers artistically on top of lettuce. Pour vinaigrette over all. Serve with **Cold Heaven Viognier**.

CONSILIENCE

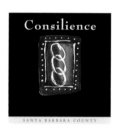

Nineteenth-century philosopher William Whewell coined the word "consilience" to describe "the coming together of knowledge among the different branches of learning." Consilience owners Tom Daughters and Brett Escalera agreed that they wanted to create a winery that would produce "consistent and approachable, premium wines," although each partner had his own vision of winemaking, quality, and service. Integrating their individual ideas represented "a coming together of knowledge" and resulted in the founding of the Santa Ynez winery that Tom and Brett aptly named "Consilience."

Brett became interested in viticulture as a child, when he watched his grandfathers make homemade wine. Years later, in the mid-1980s, Brett continued the family winemaking tradition with a part-time job in the cellar at Santa Barbara Winery. Inspired by his experience at the winery, in 1992 Brett enrolled in the enology and viticulture program at California State University, Fresno, working as a paramedic to finance his education. One late night when he delivered a patient to a Santa Barbara hospital emergency room, Brett met and befriended Tom, the resident physician, who was also a wine enthusiast.

After graduation, Brett worked for a short time at Byron Vineyard & Winery in Santa Maria, then joined the winemaking team at Fess Parker Winery & Vineyard in Los Olivos. Brett remained friends with Tom, who had gone into private practice in Santa Barbara.

One weekend, Tom and his wife, Jodie, and Brett and his wife, Monica, took a trip to Napa. By the end of the weekend the four friends had decided to establish their own winery and embark on what would become an odyssey of planning and research.

In 1997 Tom and Brett produced their first wine, a Syrah, from grapes grown in Santa Barbara County. When the wine was released in 1999, Consilience was born.

"Consilience makes small lots of premium wines loosely focused around the typical Rhône varietals," explains Brett. "We make wines for all palates, from the first-time wine taster to the connoisseur."

Consilience wines are sold in fine restaurants and retail stores throughout the United States, and in the Los Olivos tasting room, where Mambo, Tom and Jodie's black Lab, is the official greeter and mascot.

Consilience
2933 Grand Avenue
P. O. Box 529
Los Olivos, CA 93441
(805) 691-1020
info@consiliencewines.com
www.consiliencewines.com

Appellation of Origin:
Santa Barbara County

Owners:
Tom Daughters, Brett Escalera

Tasting Hours:
11 a.m. – 5 p.m. daily

Wines: Viognier, Roussanne, Grenache, Pinot Noir, Syrah, Cabernet Sauvignon, Petite Sirah, Zinfandel, Zinfandel Port, red wine blends

Winemaker's Specialty:
Petite Sirah

Winemaker: Brett Escalera

Parmesan Pork Cutlets

1 1-lb. pork tenderloin, cut into 8 pieces, pounded into 1/4-inch thickness
2 eggs, beaten
1 c. dry bread crumbs
1/4 c. Parmesan cheese, grated
1 tsp. kosher salt
1/2 c. flour
5 Tbsp. extra-virgin olive oil, divided
6 c. arugula

2 tomatoes, sliced into wedges
1 lemon, cut into four wedges

Place eggs in a small bowl and set aside. Mix bread crumbs, cheese, and salt in a shallow bowl. Dredge cutlets in flour, dip in eggs, and coat in bread-crumb mixture. Heat 2 Tbsp. oil over medium-high heat in a large skillet. Cook 4 cutlets, 1 to 2 minutes per side, until golden brown. Repeat with remaining cutlets and oil. Place cutlets on a baking sheet and bake at 400° for 8 to 10 minutes, until cooked through. Divide arugula and tomatoes on individual serving plates and drizzle with remaining oil. Place one cutlet on each plate and serve with **Consilience Santa Barbara County Syrah**.

COTTONWOOD CANYON VINEYARD & WINERY

"Distinctively different age-worthy wine," runs the motto of Cottonwood Canyon Vineyard & Winery, situated in the Santa Maria Valley amid 78 acres of estate-grown Chardonnay, Pinot Noir, and Syrah. Founded in 1988 by the Beko family, Cottonwood Canyon blends traditional Burgundian winemaking practices with modern American ingenuity to create a "hands-off" approach to winemaking. "I like to let Mother Nature deliver her flavor," says owner and winemaker Norman Beko.

Cottonwood Canyon's microclimate is often compared to the long, cool growing season of the Burgundy region of France. The slowly maturing grapes have "a high acid level that is critical to long-lived wines," explains Norman. "But unlike conditions in Burgundy, our moderate temperatures create a higher sugar level in the fruit. The grapes' high acidity also makes for unique food and wine parings."

The marriage of fine wine and food is key at Cottonwood Canyon, where guests can sample current releases with complimentary appetizers. Crackers and smoked almonds are offered with all vintages; pickled olives, asparagus, and green beans are served with Chardonnay; and a variety of cheeses accompany the red wine. To demonstrate how the pairing of wine and food influences one's wine-tasting judgment, Cottonwood Canyon's friendly staff ask visitors to take part in an unusual and amusing experiment—guests first taste wine with "an undesirable food," and then again with "the proper food."

"It's amazing how many people enjoy a certain wine when it's paired with the right food," says Norman, "a wine whose good taste was masked by the wrong food selection previously."

All wine is aged in the winery's rambling wine caves, which also provide a venue for winemaker dinners, special events, and weekend tours.

In the future, Norman plans to expand the winery to include a restaurant where guests can indulge in a *tapas*-style Thai, French, and American cuisine that complements Cottonwood Canyon's high-acid wines.

Cottonwood Canyon opened a second tasting room in Solvang in 2006.

Cottonwood Canyon Vineyard & Winery
3940 Dominion Road
Santa Maria, CA 93454
(805) 937-8463
475 First Street
Solvang, CA 93463
(805) 688-8006
cottonwoodcanyon@earthlink.net
www.cottonwoodcanyon.com

Sub-AVA: Santa Maria Valley

Owner: Norman Beko

Tasting Hours:
10 a.m. – 6 p.m. daily

Wines: Chardonnay, Pinot Noir, Syrah

Winemaker: Norman Beko

Tomato-Dill Soup

1 Tbsp. olive oil
1-1/2 c. leeks (white and pale green parts only), chopped
2 28-oz. cans diced tomatoes with juice, or the equivalent in fresh tomatoes, diced
2-1/4 c. low-salt chicken broth
3 Tbsp. fresh dill, chopped, or 1-1/2 Tbsp. dried dill
Cayenne pepper to taste
Salt and pepper to taste
1/4 c. light sour cream
3 oz. sharp white cheddar cheese, grated
Fresh dill sprigs for garnish

Heat oil in a large, heavy pot over medium heat. Add leeks and sauté until tender, about 6 minutes. Add tomatoes, broth, chopped dill, and cayenne, and bring to a boil. Reduce heat and simmer uncovered until tomatoes are very soft, about 20 minutes. Working in batches, puree soup in processor until smooth. Return soup to pot. (At this point, soup may be covered and refrigerated for one day.) Bring soup to simmer over medium-low heat. Season with salt and pepper. Gradually whisk in sour cream. Do not boil. Ladle soup into bowls, sprinkle with cheese, and garnish with dill sprigs. Serve with **Cottonwood Canyon Syroir**, a blend of Syrah and Pinot Noir.

CURTIS WINERY

For those with a passion for "all things Rhône," Firestone Family Estates' Curtis Winery is a connoisseur's delight. One of the few California wineries dedicated exclusively to Rhône varietals, Curtis crafts wines that reflect the versatility and distinct *terroir* of the Santa Ynez Valley.

Curtis wines are made in a locale with an interesting history—celebrated Hollywood television producer Douglas Cramer ("Dynasty," "Star Trek," "The Odd Couple," and "The Love Boat") owned the property in the 1980s before it became a winery. The Curtis tasting room once housed Cramer's collection of more than 600 pieces of modern art, including works by Matisse, Picasso, and Warhol. In 1995 the Firestones purchased the property that lies adjacent to Firestone Vineyards and founded Curtis Winery, named for Polly Curtis, the mother of Brooks Firestone, the founder of Firestone Vineyards.

Curtis' wines are made from the fruit of its two estate vineyards, the Ambassador's Vineyard and Crossroads Vineyard, and from limited quantities of grapes from select local vineyards. "The key to planting Rhône varietals is matching the right varietal to the right microclimate and soil type," says winemaker Chuck Carlson, who played an integral part in developing Curtis Winery and planting its vineyards.

"We harvest our grapes according to physiological ripeness, for the optimal balance between grape flavor, acid, texture, and tannin structure," Chuck explains. Curtis preserves the fruit's delicate balance with a "hands-on, pumps-off philosophy" and a traditional winemaking process that employs a classic Italian wooden basket press and gravity—not machinery—to transfer wine.

"The more you minimize the processing," says Chuck, "the more you capture a true snapshot of what's going on in the vineyard."

Curtis' sun-filled and vibrantly colored tasting room offers guests a relaxed atmosphere in which to sample current releases and purchase wine accessories, gifts, and gourmet food items made by local vendors. The winery cellar just off the tasting room offers a cozy ambience with mural-covered walls, French oak barrels, and an enormous 4,000-liter upright oak wine tank.

Curtis Winery
5249 Foxen Canyon Road
P. O. Box 244
Los Olivos, CA 93441
(805) 686-8999
info@curtiswinery.com
www.curtiswinery.com

Sub-AVA: Santa Ynez Valley

Owners:
Brooks and Kate Firestone

Tasting Hours:
10 a.m. – 5 p.m. daily

Wines: Syrah, Mourvèdre, Viognier, Roussanne, Grenache, "Heritage Series" blends

Winemaker: Chuck Carlson

Grilled Quail with Summer Salad and Sweet-Onion Vinaigrette

16 quail, boned
1 lb. thick-cut bacon
1 c. sweet-variety onion, diced
1/4 c. Muscat wine vinegar
Salt and pepper to taste
1/4 c. extra-virgin olive oil
1 lb. arugula, washed and drained
4 ears sweet corn, cut from the cob
2 pt. cherry tomatoes, heirloom varieties, halved
1/2 c. fresh chives, cut into 1/2-inch pieces

Cook bacon over medium heat until crisp. Remove bacon from pan, drain on paper towels, and break into small pieces. Pour 1/2 cup bacon fat (for vinaigrette) into a small bowl and set aside. Pour fat from pan, reserving 2 Tbsp. Sauté onion in fat until translucent and slightly browned. Add vinegar to pan and deglaze. Pour the contents of pan into a small mixing bowl. Add 1 Tbsp. cool water, and season with salt and pepper. Whisk in olive oil and add a portion of the

reserved bacon fat to desired flavor and consistency. Marinate the quail in two ounces of the vinaigrette and season with salt and pepper 1/2 hour before grilling. Grill quail over hot coals or wood to desired doneness. Toss arugula, tomatoes, and corn with remaining vinaigrette and season with salt and pepper. Place salad on plates, top with two quail, and spoon a small amount of vinaigrette over each bird. Sprinkle with bacon and chives. Serve with **Curtis Winery "The Crossroad."**

DANIEL GEHRS WINES

Daniel Gehrs became a wine enthusiast during his college years in the early 1970s, when he made small lots of wine to serve at parties. Three decades later, Dan is still making wine—as a well-respected winemaker and consultant who has influenced the California wine industry by his work for some of the most prestigious wineries in the state.

After college, Dan took an entry-level job at Paul Masson Vineyards in Saratoga, where he learned the wine business from the ground up and made what he calls his first "real wine."

"Instead of attending enology school, I decided to learn winemaking from a hands-on approach," explains Dan. "As a result, I developed an innovative, outside-the-box attitude about wine and came to my winemaking style on my own."

In 1974, in the Santa Cruz Mountains, Dan and his wife, Robin, purchased an abandoned, overgrown vineyard that they named Congress Springs Vineyard. Dan honed his winemaking skills at Congress Springs and in the mountains north of Los Gatos at Novitiate Vineyards, which he leased and operated from 1978 to 1986. In 1990 Dan sold Congress Springs and founded Daniel Gehrs Wines, and in 1993 moved with his family to Santa Barbara County.

For the next decade, while Dan made wine under his Daniel Gehrs label, he also consulted and worked for several prominent wineries, including Zaca Mesa. In 1995 Dan's first Zaca Mesa vintage, a Syrah, came in sixth on *Wine Spectator* magazine's Top 100 Wines of the Year.

Today, Daniel Gehrs Wines is a small, family-run business that makes small lots of a variety of wines. Daniel Gehrs' tasting room is the historic 1904 Heather Cottage in Los Olivos, which was built as a doctor's office and later became a private residence. The tasting room features a charming gift shop that sells wine-related accessories, specialty children's gifts, and items for the home.

Daniel Gehrs Wines
2939 Grand Avenue
P. O. Box 438
Los Olivos, CA 93441
(805) 693-9686
(800) 275-8138 toll free
info@dgwines.com
www.dgwines.com

Appellation of Origin:
Santa Barbara County

Owners: Daniel and Robin Gehrs

Tasting Hours:
11 a.m. – 6 p.m. daily

Wines: Chenin Blanc, Chardonnay, Gewürztraminer, Syrah, Pinot Noir, Grenache, Cabernet Sauvignon, Zinfandel, port, red wine blends

Winemaker's Specialties:
Chenin Blanc, Syrah

Winemaker: Daniel Gehrs

Gehrs Gazpacho

2 c. seedless red grapes
2 ripe avocados, peeled and chopped
1 c. celery, coarsely chopped
1 c. scallions, coarsely chopped
3 c. white grape juice
1-1/4 c. cucumber, peeled, seeded, and coarsely chopped
1 c. red bell pepper, coarsely chopped
1 jalapeño pepper, seeded and finely chopped
4 Tbsp. fresh lime juice
1/4 c. fresh mint leaves, chopped

Salt and white pepper to taste
Fresh mint sprigs

Coarsely puree grapes, avocados, celery, and scallions in a food processor or blender, adding grape juice as necessary to keep blade from clogging. Add cucumbers and peppers. The gazpacho should be chunky. Pour into a large bowl; add remaining grape juice, lime juice, mint, salt, and pepper. Cover and chill for 4 to 12 hours. Ladle into soup bowls, garnish with mint sprigs, and serve with **Daniel Gehrs Chenin Blanc** or **Gewürztraminer**.

EPIPHANY CELLARS

An "epiphany" is a moment of sudden intuitive understanding, a flash of insight.

When Eli Parker's family founded Fess Parker Winery & Vineyard in the Santa Ynez Valley in 1988, no one knew the new enterprise would provide Eli's epiphany, significantly altering the course of his life. Helping plant the family vineyard sparked Eli's curiosity about viticulture and launched him on a career that would reveal his stellar talent for winemaking—in 2006, Eli was named "André Tchelistcheff Winemaker of the Year" at the San Francisco International Wine Competition, America's largest and most prestigious wine competition.

Eli learned the agricultural side of winemaking in the vineyard, working long hours tending his family's vines while taking extension classes in enology from the University of California, Davis. He received a hands-on education in turning grapes into wine when he worked in the cellar at Byron Winery from 1989 to 1992.

In 1993, Eli began a three-year apprenticeship at Fess Parker with acclaimed winemaker Jed Steele—Jed would have a major influence on what would later become Eli's signature winemaking style.

Eli became head winemaker in 1996 and a year later, president of the winery (today, Eli is also director of winemaking and vineyard operations).

In 1998, Eli began an independent winemaking operation and founded Epiphany Cellars.

"Epiphany is a winemaker's winery, where I can work with my favorite varietals in small lots," explains Eli. "I can satisfy my passion for and fascination with winemaking and strive for perfection without the demands and constraints of a large operation."

At Epiphany, Eli concentrates on single-vineyard varietals with grapes from his family's and other premier Santa Barbara County vineyards, and occasionally chooses fruit grown in other counties. "I'm interested in finding unusual varietals, grapes that are interesting to work with," says Eli.

Eli's signature wine is "Revelation," a blend he makes every year with different grape varieties. "The blending of the grapes marries the different nuances of flavor," Eli says, "adding depth and complexity to the final wine."

Epiphany Cellars

2963 Grand Avenue
P. O. Box 908
Los Olivos, CA 93441
(805) 686-2424
(866) 354-9463 toll free
julie@epiphanycellars.com
www.epiphanycellars.com

Appellation of Origin:
Santa Barbara County

Owner: Eli Parker

Tasting Hours:
11:30 a.m. – 5:30 p.m.
Thursday – Monday

Wines: Pinot Gris, Roussanne, Grenache Blanc, Grenache Rosé, Grenache, Petite Sirah, Syrah

Winemaker's Specialty:
"Revelation" blend

Winemaker: Eli Parker

Louise's Two-Cheese Quiche

10 eggs, lightly beaten
1/2 c. butter
1/2 c. flour
1 Tbsp. baking powder
Dash salt
1 8-oz. can diced green chilies
1 pt. cottage cheese
1 lb. jack cheese, grated

Melt butter in a 13- by 9-inch glass baking pan. Mix eggs, flour, baking powder, and salt in a large bowl. Pour butter from baking dish into bowl and add chilies, cottage cheese, and jack cheese. Mix until just blended. Turn back into buttered baking dish. Bake at 400° for 15 minutes. Reduce heat to 350° and bake another 20 minutes or until slightly browned. (Note: Cover with aluminum foil if needed to prevent over-browning.) Serve with **Epiphany Grenache Rosé**.

FESS PARKER WINERY & VINEYARD

In the mid 1950s, Fess Parker donned a coonskin cap to play Davy Crockett in Walt Disney's weekly television show. His portrayal of the heroic pioneer catapulted Fess to international stardom and changed his life forever. Thirty years after portraying the legendary woodsman, Fess blazed a new trail by purchasing 714 acres in the Santa Ynez Valley and creating a Parker family wine tradition.

Fess Parker Winery & Vineyard was born in 1989, when Fess and his son, Eli, planted five and a half acres of Johannisberg Riesling to sell to local wineries. The initial vineyard has grown to more than 380 acres divided among Chardonnay, Pinot Noir, Syrah, and Viognier, the cornerstone varieties of the Parkers' wine production. Fess' daughter, Ashley Parker Snider, explains, "Fess is from Texas, so he can't do anything small!" By 1999, the

Parkers were annually producing 45,000 cases of ultra-premium wine that was sold in 42 states and in Canada and Japan.

Family is important to Fess and his wife, Marcy, and they take great pride that their children play integral roles in the winery's day-to-day operations. Eli is the president and director of winemaking and vineyard operations, Ashley is the marketing and public relations liaison, and son-in-law Tim Snider is vice president of sales and marketing.

The Fess Parker Winery building is one of the most impressive facilities in the Santa Ynez Valley. The expansive stone-and-wood structure resembles a hunting lodge and is surrounded by park-like grounds with tables and chairs and an inviting outdoor barbeque area.

On weekends, the former television frontiersman often visits the tasting room to sign autographs and greet guests, who can sip Fess Parker wines in glasses inscribed with Fess' famous coonskin cap. The large gift shop offers wine accessories, gourmet food items, T-shirts—and the long-tailed caps prized by several generations of Davy Crockett fans.

Fess Parker Winery & Vineyard
6200 Foxen Canyon Road
P. O. Box 908
Los Olivos, CA 93441
(805) 688-1545
(800) 841-1104 toll free
info@fessparker.com
www.fessparker.com

Sub-AVA: Santa Ynez Valley

Owners: The Parker family

Tasting Hours:
10 a.m. – 5 p.m. daily

Wines: Syrah, Viognier, Chardonnay, Pinot Noir, Riesling

Winemaker's Specialty: Syrah

Winemaker: Blair Fox

Marcy Parker's Spanish Pork Roast

2- to 3-lb. pork roast
5 cloves garlic, crushed
2 pinches oregano
1/2 tsp. cumin powder
Dash cayenne pepper
1/2 c. red wine vinegar
Salt and pepper to taste

Combine garlic, oregano, cumin, cayenne, vinegar, salt, and pepper in a small bowl. Pour mixture over roast and marinate 2 hours to overnight, basting intermittently. Place roast in a roasting pan and bake at 300° for 2-1/2 to 3 hours, or until done. Serve with **Fess Parker Rodney's Vineyard Syrah**.

FIRESTONE VINEYARD

A pioneer of the Santa Barbara County wine industry, Firestone Vineyard reflects the work of three generations of committed wine growers. The family-owned and -operated winery is the flagship enterprise of Firestone Family Estates, which comprises Firestone Vineyard, Curtis Winery, Firestone Walker Fine Ales, and Prosperity Wines.

Firestone Vineyard was born in the early 1970s when Leonard Firestone, the son of tire magnate Harvey Firestone, planted vines on the family's Santa Ynez Valley cattle ranch, with the idea of selling grapes to Northern California wineries. About the same time, Leonard's son, Brooks Firestone, decided to leave corporate life at the Firestone Tire and Rubber Company and move to the family ranch. Brooks wasn't content to sell grapes to other wineries and began researching wine and winemaking—and "never looked back." In 1972 Brooks founded the region's first estate winery, and with the guidance of Russian-born enologist and viticulturist André Tchelistcheff produced Firestone Vineyard's first vintage in 1975.

The majority of Firestone wine comes from grapes grown in its eight estate vineyards, which span a series of rocky mesas in the foothills of the Santa Ynez Valley. "The personality of the vintage can change from year to year but it's the estate fruit that gives us consistency and quality," says Brooks. "The imprint of the estate is integral to the character and individuality of our wines."

Preserving their winemaking legacy is important to the Firestones. "The multi-generational estate aspect is important to Firestone Vineyard," says Brooks. "The idea of wine representing 'people and place' goes back centuries. We subscribe to this tradition, and we think it helps create a certain magic in the bottle."

The Firestone family provides a warm, friendly, and comfortable space for their guests to explore every aspect of the winemaking experience. "Hands-on" winery tours, an elegant wood-and-stone tasting room, and picnic tables that overlook breathtaking vistas of wine country make Firestone Vineyard a "must-see" destination.

Firestone Vineyard
5000 Zaca Station Road
P. O. Box 244
Los Olivos, CA 93441
(805) 688-3940
info@firestonewine.com
www.firestonewine.com

Sub-AVA: Santa Ynez Valley

Owners: The Firestone family

Tasting Hours:
10 a.m. – 5 p.m. daily

Wines: Sauvignon Blanc, Syrah, Chardonnay, Riesling, Gewürztraminer, Merlot

Winemaker's Specialties: Sauvignon Blanc, Syrah

Winemaker: Kevin Willenborg

Shrimp, Mango, and Goat Cheese Salad

1 lb. medium shrimp without tails, cooked
4 Tbsp. fresh lime juice
1/4 tsp. salt
1/2 tsp. chili powder
2 Tbsp. plus 1 tsp. vegetable oil
1 16-oz. can black beans, rinsed and drained
1 large ripe mango, peeled and diced into small cubes
1 small red onion, finely chopped
1/3 c. goat cheese, crumbled
8 c. mixed greens

Whisk together lime juice, salt, and chili powder, then slowly add vegetable oil. Combine shrimp, beans, mango, onion, and cheese in a bowl and toss lightly with some of the dressing, reserving a portion to toss with the mixed greens. Toss greens with dressing, being careful not to over-dress. Serve with **Firestone Sauvignon Blanc** or **Gewürztraminer**.

FOLEY ESTATES VINEYARD & WINERY

"For over three thousand years man has endeavored to extract greatness from the grape. We're simply carrying on the tradition," says Bill Foley, owner of Foley Estates Vineyard & Winery in Lompoc and Lincourt Vineyards in Solvang.

Beginning in 1994, Bill produced wines at Lincourt Vineyards from grapes grown in the warm and cool climates of the Santa Ynez and Santa Maria valleys, respectively. By the late 1990s, Bill wanted to take his winemaking a step further. "I wanted to produce stellar Chardonnay and Pinot Noir, varietals that wouldn't grow in the climate near Lincourt's estate," Bill explains.

Bill enlisted the help of Lincourt winemaker Alan Phillips to search Santa Barbara County for land with the cool climate necessary to grow the fragile varietals. Bill and Alan used a systematic approach, employing topographical maps, soil research, and climatic reports.

In 1998, Bill found and purchased the perfect property, Rancho Santa Rosa, an old thoroughbred horse ranch on East Highway 246 in the Santa Rita Hills. "The property's limestone soils and steep, south-facing hillsides are considered 'the Holy Grail' to Pinot Noir and Chardonnay vintners," says Bill.

Bill and Alan divided the 460-acre property into 59 blocks, planting 118 acres of Pinot Noir on the steepest and highest terrain, 103 acres of Chardonnay on the rolling hills, and eight acres of Syrah on a south-facing, sheltered hillside.

"What's unusual about our vineyard is that although it is the largest in the Santa Rita Hills sub-AVA, we farm, harvest, and vinify as if it were 59 small separate vineyards," explains Bill.

Ten different soil types comprise the terrain, and elevations range from 430 to 1,000 feet. Bill and Alan matched each soil type with the appropriate rootstock and microclimate before planting.

Guests are invited to sample Foley's cool-climate varietals in the handsome, 3,500-square-foot stone-and-stucco tasting room and events center. Once a well-appointed stable for racehorses, the modern tasting room offers a fireplace, large windows, and a patio that overlooks manicured lawns, vineyards, and the adjacent 12,000-square-foot winery building.

Foley Estates Vineyard & Winery
6121 East Highway 246
Lompoc, CA 93436
(805) 737-6222
info@foleywines.com
www.foleywines.com

Sub-AVA: Santa Rita Hills

Owner: William "Bill" Foley II

Tasting Hours:
10 a.m. – 5 p.m. daily

Wines: Chardonnay, Pinot Noir, Syrah, Pinot Gris

Winemaker's Specialties:
Chardonnay "Barrel Select,"
Pinot Noir "Barrel Select"

Winemaker: Alan Phillips

Beef Braised in Foley Pinot Noir

4 lbs. beef chuck roast, salted to taste
2 Tbsp. extra-virgin olive oil
1 garlic clove, minced
1 red onion, finely chopped
1 stalk celery, finely chopped
4 Tbsp. herbs de Provence
1 c. Foley Estates Pinot Noir, Rancho Santa Rosa
1/2 c. brandy or cognac
1 lb. baby red potatoes

Heat oil in a large Dutch oven. Brown beef on all sides over medium heat. Add garlic, onions, celery, and herbs and cook for 5 minutes. Add wine and brandy or cognac. Reduce heat to low, cover, and cook for 1-1/2 hours. Add potatoes and cook 1 more hour, until meat is fork tender. Serve with **Foley Estates Pinot Noir, Rancho Santa Rosa.**

FOXEN WINERY & VINEYARD

Foxen Winery & Vineyard is based on a friendship that has now spanned more than 30 years, and on a 19th-century mariner's marriage and his purchase of a Spanish land grant.

Winery owners Bill Wathen and Dick Doré met in the 1970s while working at Tepusquet Mesa Vineyard. The two friends founded Foxen in 1985, on the historic Rancho Tinaquaic in northern Santa Barbara County. The land is owned by the Doré family—Dick's great-great-grandfather, English sea captain William Benjamin Foxen, came to Santa Barbara in the early 1800s, married into a Californio family, and purchased the 10,000-acre land grant. The distinctive, rustic-looking anchor Captain Foxen chose as his cattle brand is the winery's trademark and appears on all Foxen Winery & Vineyard's wine labels.

An historic barn houses the winery where Bill uses low-tech, minimalist, French-style techniques to make small lots of red wine that are aged exclusively in French oak barrels. Foxen's wines are neither fined nor filtered. Bill, who specialized in vineyard management at California Polytechnic State University and earned a degree in

fruit science, uses grapes grown in Foxen's two estate vineyards, Tinaquaic and Williamson-Doré, as well as purchased fruit from all three Santa Barbara County viticulture areas.

Adjacent to the winery stands Foxen's tasting room, a tin-roofed, open-ended building that was Dick's great-grandfather's blacksmith shop. Guests are invited to sample Foxen's vintages, browse the walls hung with historical memorabilia and photos, and view the "Foxen Shrine," a display case filled with Bill and Dick's favorite pictures and mementos. A patio with picnic tables and a second tasting bar offers a relaxing spot to admire the view of the nearby hills. Across the road stands the original homestead house where Dick was born and that in the 1800s served as a stagecoach stop.

Foxen Winery & Vineyard
7200 Foxen Canyon Road
Santa Maria, CA 93454
(805) 937-4251
info@foxenvineyard.com
www.foxenvineyard.com

Appellation of Origin:
Santa Barbara County

Owners: Bill Wathen, Dick Doré

Tasting Hours:
11 a.m. – 4 p.m. daily

Wines: Chardonnay, Old-Vine Chennin Blanc, Pinot Noir, Cabernet Sauvignon, Syrah, Bordeaux blends, Rhône-style blends

Winemaker's Specialties:
Pinot Noir, Rhône-style blends

Winemaker: Bill Wathen

Chopped Salmon with Capers Spread

1 lb. skinless salmon filets
1 c. water
1 c. white wine
1 tsp. peppercorns
1 tsp. Beau Monde seasoning
1/2 c. mayonnaise
2 Tbsp. onion, minced
2 Tbsp. capers, drained
1/2 c. parsley, chopped
1 clove garlic, minced

1 Tbsp. lemon juice
1 tsp. Dijon mustard
Salt and pepper to taste

In a large, deep skillet bring water, wine, peppercorns, and Beau Monde to a simmer. Add salmon to skillet and poach over low heat about 20 minutes, until firm. Cool. Flake fish with a fork. In a large bowl combine remaining ingredients. Gently fold in salmon. Serve with crackers and **Foxen Pinot Noir**.

GAINEY VINEYARD

Gainey Vineyard represents the work of three generations of a family that since the early 1960s has run the largest diversified farming and ranching operation in the Santa Ynez Valley. The Gainey family raises cattle and horses and grows fruit, vegetables, wheat, alfalfa, and flowers in addition to producing estate Chardonnay, Pinot Noir, Syrah, and Bordeaux varietals from its vineyards.

The family venture began in 1962, when Dan C. Gainey and his son, Dan J., purchased a 1,800-acre ranch in the eastern Santa Ynez Valley. The two Dans named their property "Home Ranch," allocating 1,000 acres to cattle, 600 to farming, and 100 to raising Arabian horses.

Two decades later, the family planted 50 acres of Bordeaux varietals to make world-class wines that would showcase the geographic and climatic diversity of the area. They also constructed a Spanish-style winery.

In the 1990s, the Gaineys extended their holdings to include 120 acres in the cooler Santa Rita Hills, and named their new property "Evan's Ranch" (Evan was the elder Gainey's father). The family planted 50 acres of cool-climate varietals, making Gainey Vineyard one of the first wineries in the Santa Ynez Valley to own vineyards in both the warm and cool parts of the valley.

"Having vineyards in two different microclimates gives us complete control of all phases of wine growing—from the planting of vines ideally suited to each vineyard site, to viticultural techniques that emphasize low yields, to winemaking that stresses minimal processing," explains Dan H. Gainey, grandson of Dan C. "Both properties are self-sufficient operations."

Gainey Vineyard's visitor-friendly tasting room easily accommodates large groups and hosts many special events, including winemaker dinners, cooking classes, weddings, private parties, and an annual crush party. Outdoor summer concerts are held in the circular courtyard that is shaded by sycamore trees and surrounded by vineyards and a majestic panorama of mountains.

The Gainey family invites guests to enjoy the picnic area adjacent to the tasting room and to take one of the daily guided tours to learn more about the family's wine-growing, farming, and ranching enterprise.

Gainey Vineyard
3950 East Highway 246
Santa Ynez, CA 93460
(805) 688-0558
info@gaineyvineyard.com
www.gaineyvineyard.com

Sub-AVAs: Santa Ynez Valley, Santa Rita Hills

Owners: The Gainey family

Tasting Hours:
10 a.m. – 5 p.m. daily

Wines: Sauvignon Blanc, Chardonnay, Riesling, Merlot, Pinot Noir, Syrah

Winemaker's Specialty: "Limited Selection" wines

Winemaker: Kirby Anderson

Filet of Sole with Capers, Almonds, and Lemon

8 3-oz. sole filets
1 c. all-purpose flour
Salt and freshly ground pepper to taste
3-1/2 Tbsp. unsalted butter, divided
2 Tbsp. canola oil
1/4 c. slivered almonds
1/4 c. capers, drained
1 small lemon, sliced paper-thin

Place flour in a shallow dish, add salt and pepper, and mix. Dredge fish filets in flour mixture and place on a plate; set aside. Melt 1 Tbsp. butter and 1 Tbsp. oil in a large skillet. Add half of the filets and cook over high heat, turning once, 3 to 4 minutes, until golden and crisp. Transfer to a platter, cover with foil, and keep warm. Repeat procedure with remaining filets. Add remaining 1-1/2 Tbsp. butter and almonds to the skillet. Cook over high heat for 2 minutes, stirring until golden brown. Add capers and lemon slices and cook 1 minute until heated through. Spoon sauce over the fish and serve with **Gainey Vineyard Limited Selection Sauvignon Blanc**.

HITCHING POST WINES

One of America's best-known wineries is Hitching Post Wines, whose tasting room at the Hitching Post restaurant in Buellton appeared in "Sideways," the 2004 hit film that received five Academy Award nominations and an Oscar.

Winery owners Gray Hartley and Frank Ostini became friends in 1976. Gray was a fisherman who had purchased the house behind the Ostini family's original Hitching Post restaurant in Casmalia. Three years later, Frank decided to make wine to complement the restaurant's cuisine and asked Gray to join him as winemaker in the new business venture. At the time, Gray knew nothing about winemaking but he accepted Frank's offer, and the two embarked on a shared career that would one day make their winery known around the world.

The new winemaking partners made their first vintage, a Merlot, in Frank's garage in 1979. Frank and Gray followed with a Cabernet Sauvignon in 1980, and a Pinot Noir in 1981.

"We became smitten with Pinot Noir right away," remembers Gray. "We were enamored with the wonderful and mysterious woman in the form of a delectable grape cluster."

In 1986 Frank opened the second Hitching Post restaurant in Buellton, which serves as the tasting room for Hitching Post Wines.

Today, Gray and Frank make wine at a Santa Maria commercial winery with grapes purchased from premium Santa Barbara County growers. They employ a minimalist approach to winemaking: They cold soak the grapes for two days, add cultured yeast to promote a long, cool fermentation, and manually punch down the grape-skin caps one to three times per day. Grapes are pressed 14 to 21 days after fermentation and the juice goes directly into barrels—mostly French oak—where it ages *sur lie* for about 18 months. The wine is raked just before bottling and is only fined and/or filtered when needed.

"Being a romantic soul, I allow the vineyard to speak clearly, singing the song it was meant to sing," says Gray. "I'm not an interventionist who needs to put his signature on the wine."

Hitching Post Wines
406 East Highway 246
Buellton, CA 93427
(805) 688-0676
info@hitchingpostwines.com
www.hitchingpost2.com

Appellation of Origin:
Santa Barbara County

Owners:
Gray Hartley, Frank Ostini

Tasting Hours:
4 p.m. – 6 p.m. daily

Wines: Pinot Noir, Merlot, Syrah, Cabernet Franc, red wine blends

Winemakers' Specialty:
"Highliner" Pinot Noir

Winemakers:
Gray Hartley, Frank Ostini

Santa Maria-Style Oakwood-Grilled Beef Rib Chops

3 rib chop steaks (cut from the prime rib, about 2 lbs.)
1/2 c. red-wine vinegar
1/2 c. garlic-infused vegetable oil
2 tsp. freshly ground black pepper
2 tsp. white pepper
2 tsp. Cayenne pepper
1 tsp. onion powder
4 Tbsp. granulated garlic
6 Tbsp. salt

Prepare barbeque grill, using oakwood instead of charcoal. Mix vinegar and oil in a small bowl. Combine all dry ingredients in another bowl. Baste and season both sides of steaks with oil-and-vinegar and dry-ingredient mixtures. Place chops on a low- to medium-temperature fire. Cook approximately 6 to 8 minutes, turning as each side gets crispy and before the heat releases juices, basting and seasoning lightly 3 or 4 times per side after turning. Grill until chops are cooked to your liking. Remove from fire and let rest for 10 minutes before cutting into 1/2-inch slices on an angle against the grain. Serve with **Hitching Post "Highliner" Pinot Noir**.
Recipe courtesy Frank Ostini and the Hitching Post Restaurants

(Photos courtesy Craig Jaffurs)

JAFFURS WINE CELLARS

One of Santa Barbara County's first producers of Viognier and Syrah, Jaffurs Wine Cellars makes handcrafted Rhône-style wines in its downtown Santa Barbara winery.

Owner and winemaker Craig Jaffurs moved to the West Coast from his native Maryland in the mid-1970s to attend the University of California, San Francisco. After graduation, he relocated to Santa Barbara, where he began a career as an aerospace cost analyst.

By the late 1980s, Craig realized that working in the aerospace industry wasn't what he wanted to do for the rest of his life. Craig's plans for a career change crystallized when he befriended Bruce McGuire, the winemaker at Santa Barbara Winery. A longtime wine aficionado, Craig offered to help Bruce with harvests at the winery in exchange for a hands-on education in winemaking. Craig also pursued wine studies on his own, reading books, making wine in his garage, and enrolling in several enology extension classes through the University of California, Davis.

In 1994, Craig left his job as a cost analyst and founded Jaffurs Wine Cellars, making wine at Central Coast Wine Services in Santa Maria from purchased grapes grown in Santa Barbara County. Craig's efforts soon went beyond working with the harvested fruit as he became closely involved in viticulture.

"We custom farm blocks of several premier vineyards and control all aspects of production, from crop yield to harvest," explains Craig.

Jaffurs' first release, a 1994 Santa Barbara County Syrah, received a rating of 91 points from *Wine Spectator* magazine and 90 from *Robert J. Parker Jr.'s The Wine Advocate*.

In 2001, Craig completed construction of a 3,000-square-foot state-of-the-art climate-controlled winery on East Montecito Street. The winery contains a walk-in cooler as well as ample wall space for Craig—an avid surfer—to display his collection of surfboards.

"We're a surf-oriented working winery by day and a tasting room by weekend," Craig says of the winery, where Friday through Sunday guests sample Jaffurs' current releases at a table set up in the barrel room.

Jaffurs Wine Cellars
819 East Montecito Street
Santa Barbara, CA 93103
(805) 962-7003
info@jaffurswine.com
www.jaffurswine.com

Appellation of Origin:
Santa Barbara County

Owners:
Craig Jaffurs, Lee Wardlaw Jaffurs

Tasting Hours:
Noon – 4 p.m. Friday – Sunday
And by appointment

Wines: Viognier, Roussanne, Syrah, Petite Sirah, Grenache

Winemaker's Specialty: Syrah

Winemaker: Craig Jaffurs

Craig's Smoked Salmon with Cucumber-Dill Sauce

2-3 lbs. 1-inch thick salmon steaks
  or filets, scored

Brine
2 c. soy sauce
2 c. Jaffurs Viognier or Roussanne
1/4 c. minced onions
1/2 tsp. ground black pepper
1 Tbsp. minced garlic
1/2 tsp. hot pepper sauce
1/3 c. sugar
1/4 c. non-ionized salt

Sauce
1 cucumber, peeled, seeded, and sliced
1/2 c. sour cream
1/2 tsp. dill, or to taste

Mix brine ingredients. Place salmon in a large, shallow glass or plastic container and pour brine over salmon. Cover, refrigerate, and let marinate overnight (12 to 16 hours).

Remove salmon from brine and pat dry. Place salmon on a rack and allow to air dry for an hour or until a slight glaze forms. Place salmon on rack in smoker at about 110°. Smoke with alder or other mild wood for 3 hours. (Note: Do not use oak.) Leave fish in warm smoker for 6 to 8 more hours without smoke.

Mix cucumber, sour cream, and dill and puree in a food processor until smooth. Serve salmon warm with cucumber-dill sauce and **Jaffurs Syrah**.

KALYRA WINERY

Kalyra Winery is known as "the little winery with the big personality," a description which reflects the outgoing natures of owner-winemaker Mike Brown and his brother, general manager Martin Brown. *Dining Out* magazine named the native Australians "among the friendliest hosts in the Santa Ynez Valley," emphasizing that "a visit to their winery is always fun."

"Kalyra" is the Australian Aboriginal word for "a wild and pleasant place" and the Browns have designed their tasting room to resemble an outback beach shack: a surfboard hangs on the wall, and the gift shop features arts and crafts made by indigenous peoples from around the world.

Mike was introduced to wine growing at an early age, when he worked at his family's vineyard in Australia. Later, he attended the University of Adelaide, where he received undergraduate degrees in microbiology and pharmacology. After graduation, he came to the United States and the University of California, Davis, to earn a master's degree in enology and viticulture—and to surf.

"I was captivated by the beaches and breaks off the Santa Barbara coast," Mike explains. "I took a job at a Santa Maria winery so I could surf on my days off."

For the next few years, Mike made wine, surfed, and in California's "off season" returned to Australia to help with the harvest at his family's vineyard.

In the early 1970s, Mike moved to Santa Barbara, where for the next two decades he gained winemaking experience at several local wineries, including Zaca Mesa, Mosby, Buttonwood Farm, and Santa Ynez. In 1989, Mike ventured out on his own, founding Kalyra Winery.

Kalyra specializes in wine made from grapes grown in Santa Barbara County—particularly the Santa Ynez Valley—and in Monterey, Amador, and Madera counties. Mike also blends Australian and California varietals to make a variety of wines from "down under." He believes "wine should exhibit the flavors of the fruit and should highlight the distinct varietal characteristics of the regions the grapes come from."

In 1997, Mike and Martin launched the M. Brown label, bottling wine from their native Australia and offering it to guests at Kalyra Winery's surf-shack tasting room.

Kalyra Winery
343 Refugio Road
Santa Ynez, CA 93460
(805) 693-8864
info@kalyrawinery.com
www.kalyrawinery.com

Sub-AVA: Santa Ynez Valley

Owner: Mike Brown

Tasting Hours:
11 a.m. – 5 p.m. Monday – Friday
10 a.m. – 5 p.m. Saturday – Sunday

Wines: Sauvignon Blanc, Chardonnay, Pinot Grigio, Cabernet Sauvignon, Bordeaux-style blends, sparkling wines, dessert wines

Winemaker's Specialties: Port, fortified dessert wines

Winemaker: Mike Brown

Mustard-Dill Pork Chops

6 pork chops, cut 1 inch thick
3 to 4 Tbsp. Dijon mustard
1 Tbsp. unsalted butter
1 Tbsp. olive oil
1 large onion, thinly sliced
3 Tbsp. flour
1-1/2 c. chicken broth
3/4 c. whole milk (or low- or non-fat)
1 tsp. freshly snipped dill
1/2 tsp. salt
1/2 tsp. white pepper
Cooked basmati rice

Generously brush one side of chops with mustard. Melt butter and oil in a large, heavy skillet. Add chops, mustard side down, and cook over medium heat until lightly browned. Brush top side with mustard, turn, and cook until lightly browned. Remove chops, keep warm. Add onions to pan and cook until golden brown, about 5 to 10 minutes. Remove skillet from heat, add flour, and whisk to combine. Add broth, a little at a time, whisking constantly to prevent lumps from forming. Return pan to heat and cook until boiling. Add milk and stir. Add dill, salt, and pepper.

Return chops to pan, reduce heat, cover, and simmer for 50 to 60 minutes, until tender, turning once. Serve chops with sauce over hot rice and **Kalyra Pinot Grigio.**

KENNETH VOLK VINEYARDS

Before Ken Volk established Kenneth Volk Vineyards he had a successful 25-year career in San Luis Obispo County, where he founded Wild Horse Vineyards and served as its winemaker.

Ken became interested in winemaking in the late 1970s, when he was a fruit science student at California Polytechnic State University in San Luis Obispo.

"A friend gave me a small lot of Gamay grapes and I made my first wine in a trash can with a baseball bat," remembers Ken. "I was hooked."

His first winemaking experience prompted Ken to read numerous wine and viticulture publications and to take enology extension courses from the University of California, Davis, as well as technical classes at the Napa School of Cellaring.

In 1981 Ken founded Wild Horse Vineyards. After selling his winery, in 2003 he purchased the original Byron Winery facility in the Santa Maria Valley (Byron had moved to new quarters). The property included a four-acre Chardonnay vineyard planted in 1981. Ken named his new venture Kenneth Volk Vineyards and released his first vintage in 2006.

"I'm not trying to redo what I've done in the past," Ken emphasizes. "I want to raise the bar and create a portfolio of luxury wines."

Kenneth Volk Vineyards produces world-class Burgundian-style wines from grapes grown in the Santa Maria Valley and Bordeaux-style varieties with fruit from the west side of Paso Robles in San Luis Obispo County. Ken's specialties are Chardonnay and Pinot Noir, which he makes from the harvests of premier Santa Maria Valley vineyards, many of which are within a six-mile radius of his winery.

"Our winery is adjacent to some of the top Pinot Noir and Chardonnay vineyards in Santa Barbara County," explains Ken. "Because of our close proximity, we are able to harvest the fruit, take it to the winery, and get it into the tanks right away."

Ken describes himself as "an innovative traditionalist winemaker" who uses progressive techniques to minimize the handling of the fruit and wine.

Grapes are crushed in a pressure-regulated basket press connected to a computer. Oxygen contact with the aging wine is kept to a minimum—barrels are manually rotated on wheeled racks to keep the lees in suspension, eliminating the need to open the bung and stir the wine by hand.

Kenneth Volk Vineyards
5230 Tepusquet Road
Santa Maria, CA 93454
(805) 938-7896
info@volkwines.com
www.volkwines.com

Sub-AVA: Santa Maria Valley

Owners: Kenneth and Tricia Volk

Tasting Hours:
10:30 a.m. – 4:30 p.m.
Friday – Sunday

Wines: Chardonnay, Viognier, Pinot Blanc, Malvasiz Blanca, Pinot Noir, Cabernet Sauvignon, Merlot, Zinfandel, Mourvèdre, Syrah

Winemaker's Specialties: Chardonnay, Pinot Noir

Winemaker: Kenneth Volk

Crostini with Mushrooms

12 1/2-inch-thick slices Italian country-style bread
10 oz. fresh porcini, shitake, or button mushrooms (or a combination of all), sliced
3 Tbsp. extra-virgin olive oil
3 whole cloves garlic, peeled
12 thin slices fontina cheese
Salt and freshly ground pepper to taste

Preheat oven to 350°. Place bread on a baking sheet and toast in oven, turning once, until barely golden, about 6 minutes. Let cool. Heat oil and garlic in a frying pan. Add mushrooms and sauté over high heat, stirring a few times, about 5 minutes. Add salt and pepper and remove pan from heat. Arrange cheese slices on top of toast. Just before serving, top with mushrooms and bake until cheese starts to melt, about 4 minutes. Arrange on a platter and serve immediately with **Kenneth Volk Pinot Noir** or **Chardonnay**.

KOEHLER WINERY

Just northwest of the picturesque town of Los Olivos, Koehler Winery makes its home amid the lush vegetation of Foxen Canyon. The previous owner of the 100-acre property sold the fruit of his 30-year-old vines to local wineries that consistently garnered accolades in national and international wine competitions. Koehler purchased the property in 1997 to create premium estate wines from the award-winning grapes.

Koehler Winery takes pride in making affordable estate wines from its 67-acre vineyard planted to Cabernet Sauvignon, Chardonnay, Sauvignon Blanc, Riesling, Syrah, Sangiovese, Grenache, Cabernet Franc, and Viognier. Pinot Noir is made from fruit purchased in the Santa Rita Hills.

"The winemaking philosophy at Koehler is based on the belief that everything in nature is in balance," says winemaker Chris Stanton. "I work closely with the vineyard manager to use cultivation techniques that are ecologically friendly. This approach results in quality fruit that allows us to create wines to please all palates."

Koehler's winemaking team oversees every step of production, from bud break to bottling. Wines are aged in the traditional style, in both old and new French oak barrels, and are not released until ready to drink.

Wine aficionados can taste Koehler's current offerings at the winery's comfortable tasting room or in the shade of the large trees that grow in the quiet adjoining garden. Guests are invited to bring sack lunches to enjoy with a bottle of Koehler wine at the outdoor picnic tables—and to visit with the "rescued animals" sheltered on the property. In Koehler's peaceable kingdom, emus form the welcoming committee at the winery's entrance, friendly cats and dogs wander the generous grounds, and Barbados sheep graze on the hill behind the tasting room.

Koehler Winery
5360 Foxen Canyon Road
P.O. Box 837
Los Olivos, CA 93441
(805) 693-8384
info@koehlerwinery.com
www.koehlerwinery.com

Sub-AVA: Santa Ynez Valley

Tasting Hours:
10 a.m. – 5 p.m. daily

Wines: Chardonnay, Sauvignon Blanc, Sangiovese, Syrah, Cabernet Sauvignon, Viognier, Grenache, Pinot Noir

Winemaker's Specialties: Chardonnay, Syrah

Winemaker: Chris Stanton

Dave's Grilled Rainbow Trout with Rosemary

4 8- to 10-oz. rainbow trout boneless filets ("ruby-red" flesh only)
2 Tbsp. dried rosemary
1 Tbsp. dried sage leaves
1/2 tsp. celery salt
1/2 tsp. ground pepper
Olive oil
Juice from 1 large lemon

Rub both sides of fish filets with olive oil and sprinkle flesh side with 1 Tbsp. rosemary, sage leaves, celery salt, and pepper. Fold a large piece of heavy-duty aluminum foil in half, poke holes with a fork, grease foil with olive oil, and place on hot grill. Sprinkle flesh side of filets with half of the lemon juice *just 30 seconds* before placing on grill. Place fish, flesh side down, on the foil. Grill 3 to 4 minutes on each side until fish flakes with a fork. Use a greased spatula to remove. Sprinkle with remaining lemon juice and rosemary and serve immediately with **Koehler Chardonnay**.

Recipe courtesy David S. Harmon, Colorado fisherman and chef

LAFOND WINERY & VINEYARD

LAFOND
2004
PINOT NOIR
SANTA RITA HILLS
SRH

When longtime Santa Barbara County wine producer Pierre Lafond founded Lafond Winery & Vineyard in 1998, he was crowning an already distinguished winemaking career that had spanned more than 30 years. In 1962, Pierre had established the downtown-based Santa Barbara Winery, the first winery in Santa Barbara County since Prohibition.

Pierre had two objectives in founding Lafond: He wanted to build a winery and tasting room next to his vineyards in the Santa Rita Hills, and to underscore the personal care and craft he brings to his winemaking—labels on his earlier wines carried only the name "Santa Barbara Winery."

Located 18 miles from the Pacific Ocean, Lafond Winery & Vineyard is ideally suited for the cool-climate varietals Lafond is well-known for—Pinot Noir, Syrah, and Chardonnay. Winemaker Bruce McGuire explains, "The long, cool summers consistently extend the growing season, producing grapes of great depth and superior extraction." Bruce believes that great wine begins in the vineyard, where leaf thinning and canopy management are an integral part of the grape-growing process.

All of Lafond's harvest undergoes a three-step selection process before crushing: Grapes are selectively picked in the field, inspected as they are placed in bins, and then pass a final inspection before the conveyor belt sends them through the de-stemming and crushing apparatus. A shaking stainless steel screen de-stems the fruit and prevents the "jacks" (the grapes' small, short stems), unripened berries, and any undesirable small particles from falling into the fermentation vat.

Bruce makes small quantities of high-end, reserve-style wines that reflect the most concentrated and intense characteristics of Lafond's fruit. He says he often envisions his favorite dishes when crafting a particular wine so the special vintage and entrée can be enjoyed together.

The Lafond tasting room boasts a spectacular view of the vineyard and hills and is available for small private events and weddings.

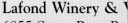

Lafond Winery & V
6855 Santa Rosa Ro
Buellton, CA 93427
(805) 688-7921
(877) 708-9463 toll free
wine@sbwinery.com
www.lafondwinery.com

Sub-AVA: Santa Rita Hills

Owner: Pierre Lafond

Tasting Hours:
10 a.m. – 5 p.m. daily

Wines: Chardonnay, Pinot Noir, Syrah

Winemaker's Specialties:
Pinot Noir, cool-climate Syrah

Winemaker: Bruce McGuire

Grilled Mushrooms and Arugula Salad

4 portobello or 8 large shitake mushrooms
1/2 c. "fruity" olive oil
Splash balsamic vinegar
2 cloves garlic, sliced
1 tsp. fresh thyme leaves
Salt and freshly ground pepper
Fresh rosemary sprigs
Arugula salad greens
Parmesan cheese, shaved

Mix olive oil and vinegar. Place mushrooms in a shallow bowl and brush sparingly with oil/balsamic mixture. Sprinkle with garlic, thyme, salt, and pepper. Lay rosemary sprigs on top of mushrooms. Cover loosely and chill for 24 hours.

Prepare hot coals for grilling and grease grill. Dampen rosemary sprigs with water and place on coals. Arrange mushrooms on grill (gill side down), cover, and cook for 4 minutes. Turn and cook another 4 minutes, uncovered. Place on top of arugula and sprinkle with Parmesan. Serve with **Lafond Pinot Noir** or **Chardonnay**.

LINCOURT VINEYARDS

Lincourt Vineyards in Solvang is the sister winery of Foley Estates Vineyard & Winery in Lompoc. Both wineries were established by Bill Foley, the founder and chief executive officer of Fidelity National Financial Corporation, one of the largest title insurance companies in America.

Bill was a longtime wine enthusiast and in 1994 he and his wife, Carol, and their four children moved to Santa Barbara. "I wanted to fulfill my dream of creating Burgundian-style wines that showcase the ideal grape-growing conditions of Santa Barbara County," Bill explains.

Bill purchased an old dairy farm on Alamo Pintado Road—the property included a 1926 Craftsman-style farmhouse built from a Sears mail-order catalogue kit. Bill converted the two milking barns to a winery and barrel room and the farmhouse to a tasting room. The Foleys named their new venture "Lincourt," blending the names of their daughters, Lindsay and Courtney.

Lincourt makes wine from its estate grapes as well as those grown at the Solomon Hills, Bien Nacido, and Star Lane vineyards. "These are some of the great vineyards of the Santa Maria and Santa Ynez valleys," Bill emphasizes. "The owners are among the county's most fastidious growers, people who share our goal of extremely low yields and ripe sugars balanced by crisp acidity."

Bill believes Lincourt wines represent the best estate fruit of Santa Barbara County and reflect the diverse

regional and varietal personality of the area: "Our style of Chardonnay and Pinot Noir speak the various appellations and vineyards that we contract premium fruit from."

Winemaker Alan Phillips employs classic winemaking principles, including whole-cluster crush for Chardonnay and hand punch-down for Pinot Noir. "I continually strive to 'coax' the greatest complexity out of the grapes," says Alan.

Lincourt's tasting room has the feel of an old, comfortable home and is surrounded by lush lawns and gardens. It is an enchanting place to picnic and spend the day and to appreciate the serenity and romance of a simpler time when a dairyman could order an attractive, do-it-yourself house through the mail.

Lincourt Vineyards
1711 Alamo Pintado Road
Solvang, CA 93463
(805) 688-8554
info@lincourtwines.com
www.lincourtwines.com

Sub-AVA: Santa Ynez Valley

Owner: William "Bill" Foley II

Tasting Hours:
10 a.m. – 5 p.m. daily

Wines: Chardonnay, Sauvignon Blanc, Pinot Noir, Syrah, Merlot

Winemaker's Specialty: "Bien Nacido Vineyard" Chardonnay

Winemaker: Alan Phillips

Beer-Battered Coconut Shrimp with Sweet Ginger Dressing and Glaze

1-1/2 lbs. shrimp, shelled, de-veined, tails removed
2 eggs, beaten
3/4 c. coconut milk
1-1/2 c. beer
1 tsp. cilantro, finely chopped
Juice from 1/2 lime
1/3 tsp. each cayenne pepper, dried oregano leaves, lemongrass
1/6 tsp. each paprika, garlic powder, white pepper
1/2 c. shredded coconut
1 c. flour
1 Tbsp. baking powder

1-1/2 Tbsp. honey
Peanut oil
Shredded coconut, browned, for garnish
1 Tbsp. prepared sweet-and-sour sauce

Mix eggs, coconut milk, beer, cilantro, and lime juice in a large bowl. Stir in cayenne, oregano, lemongrass, paprika, garlic powder, and white pepper. Add shrimp to bowl, stir to coat. Cover bowl and refrigerate at least 30 minutes. Mix coconut, flour, and baking powder in a medium bowl. Remove shrimp from refrigerator and gently fold in coconut-flour mixture. Place battered shrimp on a large plate and drizzle with honey. Heat oil in a large, deep skillet. Brown shrimp and drain on paper towels. Brown additional shredded coconut for garnish. Drizzle with sweet-and-sour sauce. Serve with **Lincourt Sauvignon Blanc, Santa Barbara County**.

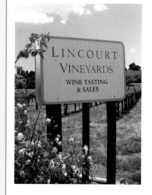

RICHARD LONGORIA
WINES
TASTING & SALES
ARTISTRY IN WINEMAKING SINCE 1982

LONGORIA
WINES
WINE TASTING

OPEN

LONGORIA WINES

"My goal has always been to discover the *grand cru*—the top-ranking—vineyards in Santa Barbara County and to work with their owners to grow the best possible grapes every year," says Longoria Wines owner Rick Longoria. "Using my experience and artisan approach to winemaking, I strive to produce the highest quality wines."

Rick's winemaking career began in 1974 at a Sonoma winery, where he befriended and worked with André Tchelistcheff, the legendary Russian-born enologist viticulturist who is considered America's most influential post-Prohibition winemaker.

In 1976, Rick moved to Santa Barbara County and became cellar foreman at Firestone Vineyard in Santa Ynez. By 1982, Rick felt assured in his winemaking skills and founded Longoria Wines, specializing in Chardonnay and Pinot Noir made from grapes grown in the Santa Maria Valley.

For the next 15 years, Rick produced small amounts of wine under the Longoria label while working at some of Santa Barbara County's most acclaimed wineries.

"In December of 1997, I gave up steady employment to give all my energies to my own business," Rick recalls. Five months later, Rick and his wife, Diana, opened the doors to the Longoria Wines tasting room in Los Olivos.

Today, Longoria Wines is a small, family-run winery that makes very limited amounts of handcrafted wines from grapes grown at the Sanford & Benedict and Fe Ciega vineyards in the Santa Rita Hills and the Bien Nacido Vineyard in the Santa Maria Valley. Rick has no desire to grow Longoria Wines into a large-scale operation—he wants to maintain a hands-on approach and make the wine himself, the part of wine growing he enjoys the most.

The Longoria tasting room makes its home in one of Los Olivos' oldest buildings, an early 20th-century structure that was originally a machine shop. Guests may sample Longoria's current offerings at the oak-paneled tasting bar or in the patio garden among roses, fruit trees, and climbing jasmine.

Longoria Wines
2935 Grand Avenue, Suite B
P. O. Box 186
Los Olivos, CA 93441
(805) 688-0305
(866) 759-4637 toll free
info@longoriawine.com
www.longoriawine.com

Appellation of Origin:
Santa Barbara County

Owners: Rick and Diana Longoria

Tasting Hours:
Noon – 4:30 p.m. Mon., Wed., Thurs.
11 a.m. – 4:30 p.m. Friday – Sunday

Wines: Chardonnay, Pinot Noir, Cabernet Franc, Syrah, Grenache, Merlot, Pinot Grigio

Winemaker's Specialties:
Fe Ciega Vineyard Pinot Noir, "Blues" Cuvée

Winemaker: Rick Longoria

Manhattan Clam Linguine

16 oz. linguine
2 qt. plus 3-1/2 c. water
3 6-1/2 oz. cans minced clams, drained, liquid
    reserved
2 Tbsp. plus 1/2 tsp. salt, divided
4 Tbsp. butter
4 Tbsp. fresh parsley, snipped
6 cloves garlic, finely chopped
3 tsp. dried sweet basil leaves
1/2 tsp. dried thyme leaves
Dash ground pepper
1 c. whipping cream

1/2 c. Longoria Chardonnay
1/2 c. Parmesan cheese, grated

Bring water, clam liquid, and 2 Tbsp. salt to a boil in a large pot. Add linguine; cook uncovered 8 to 10 minutes, stirring occasionally until just tender. Drain. Melt 4 Tbsp. butter in a 2-quart saucepan. Stir in parsley, garlic, basil, thyme, pepper, and clams. Cook over low heat, stirring, until clams are heated through. Heat cream and wine, stirring constantly, to boiling in a 1-quart saucepan. Boil and stir 1 minute. Pour over clam mixture. Place hot linguine on a platter, pour sauce over all, and toss. Garnish with Parmesan cheese and serve with **Longoria Chardonnay**.

LUCAS & LEWELLEN VINEYARDS & WINERY

Lucas & Lewellen Vineyards & Winery in Solvang is down the street from Mandolina Winery—both wineries are owned by Louis Lucas, a fourth-generation grape grower, and Royce Lewellen, a retired superior court judge. Lucas & Lewellen was founded when Louis and Royce joined forces to produce Rhône, Bordeaux, and Burgundian varietals and begin what they call their "adventure in winemaking."

In 1947, Louis and his family moved from Croatia to Delano, California, where they established a vineyard and became top producers of table grapes. Twenty years later, Louis and his brothers expanded the family's vineyard holdings, buying acreages in Santa Maria, Paso Robles, and the Edna Valley in San Luis Obispo and planting vineyards whose fruit they sold to premium Northern California wineries.

"By 1996, I was ready to step out from behind the scenes and make my own wine," explains Louis. One day over lunch, Louis asked his friend, Royce, to become co-owner in a business venture to make wine. The new co-partnership included Louis' vineyards in Santa Maria and Los Alamos and two new properties that Louis and Royce purchased together—one in Santa Ynez and another in Los Alamos. Together, these vineyards would supply grapes for the newly founded Lucas & Lewellen winery and other premier wineries.

In 1999, Louis and Royce hired veteran winemaker Daniel Gehrs, who began his viticulture career in the early 1970s at Paul Masson in Northern California and in 1990 established his own brand, Daniel Gehrs Wines. In 2000, Lucas & Lewellen released its first estate wines to rave reviews.

Today, Lucas & Lewellen grows Pinot Noir and Chardonnay in its Santa Maria vineyards; Rhône, Burgundian, Bordeaux, and Italian varietals in its Los Alamos vineyards; and Cabernet Sauvignon and Cabernet Franc in Santa Ynez.

Two wine clubs showcase Lucas & Lewellen wines: the Lucas & Lewellen Wine Club, which sends flagship wines to members, and the Owner's Selection Wine Club, whose members receive reserve wines from the library collection.

Lucas & Lewellen Vineyards & Winery
1645 Copenhagen Drive
Solvang, CA 93463
(805) 686-9336
(888) 777-6663 toll free
info@llwine.com
www.llwine.com

Appellation of Origin:
Santa Barbara County

Owners:
Louis Lucas, Royce Lewellen

Tasting Hours:
11 a.m. – 5:30 p.m. daily

Wines: Chardonnay, Viognier, Riesling, Late Harvest Sauvignon Blanc, Pinot Noir, Cabernet Sauvignon, Cabernet Franc, Syrah, Petite Sirah, sparkling wine

Winemaker's Specialty:
Cabernet Franc

Winemaker: Daniel Gehrs

Bittersweet Molten Chocolate Mini-Cakes

4 oz. bittersweet baking chocolate
4 Tbsp. butter
1 large egg
1/3 c. sugar
Pinch of salt
1 Tbsp. flour

Preheat the oven to 350°F. Melt chocolate and butter together in a small saucepan. Whisk the egg, sugar, and salt together until yellow and light. Fold in melted chocolate and butter mixture. Mix in the flour until fully incorporated. Lightly butter four cupcake tins. Pour batter into tins and bake for about 12 minutes, just until the tops crack. Using oven mitts, place foil on top of the cupcake tin and seal on all sides. Turn cupcake tin upside down onto a flat surface and tap bottom of tin to release cakes. Lift cupcake tin, leaving cakes upside down on foil. Carefully turn cakes right side up and place on individual serving plates. Serve warm with **Lucas & Lewellen Cabernet Sauvignon**.

(Photo courtesy Lucas & Lewellen Vineyards & Winery)

MANDOLINA WINERY

"We think the Italian grapes we grow make great wines that stand on their own," says Louis Lucas, who with partner Royce Lewellen founded Solvang's Mandolina Winery in 2002 to showcase their Cal-Italian varietals.

Louis and Royce created Mandolina as a second label for their successful Lucas & Lewellen Vineyards & Winery, established in 1996. For two years Mandolina, which is separately bonded, shared tasting-room quarters with Lucas & Lewellen on Copenhagen Drive, until 2004, when a new facility exclusively for Mandolina was opened just down the street.

"We wanted to call special attention to Mandolina and the Cal-Italian varietals that we were making," explains Louis.

Mandolina makes a variety of wines, including Pinot Grigio, Barbera, and Dolcetto. "Dolcetto is the everyday drinking wine for those who love food," says Louis. "I call it 'wash down' wine. You eat a lot of food and you wash it down!"

Growing Italian varietals has always been a favorite pursuit for Louis. He oversees all viticulture operations and personally selects the grapes at the Los Alamos Valley Vineyards, planted with cuttings from some of Italy's best vineyards.

"Our Italian varietals thrive in the Los Alamos Valley, where warm summer days and cool coastal nights provide the perfect growing environment."

Mandolina's colorful, Tuscan-style tasting room features a variety of gourmet packaged foods, wine-related items, paintings, and Italian gifts. Louis and Royce encourage visitors to "sit and relax and become one of the family."

"Growing grapes and making wine requires personal attention," Louis emphasizes. "If you can pass on that personal attention to consumers, you create a brand and a name that people will look for when they shop for fine wine. I often hear that someone has had a great experience at our tasting rooms and has sent friends to sample our wines. It's the best compliment we can receive."

Louis and Royce established the Mandolina Wine Club to offer members the convenience of receiving Mandolina wines at home.

Mandolina Winery
1665 Copenhagen Drive
Solvang, CA 93463
(805) 686-5506
(888) 777-6663 toll free
info@mandolinawines.com
www.mandolinawines.com

Appellation of Origin:
Santa Barbara County

Owners:
Louis Lucas, Royce Lewellen

Tasting Hours:
11 a.m. – 5:30 p.m. daily

Wines: Pinot Grigio, Barbera, Nebbiolo, Moscato, Sangiovese, Super-Tuscan blends, Dolcetto

Winemaker's Specialty:
Super-Tuscan blends

Winemaker: Daniel Gehrs

Insalata del Fagiolo con Spinaci ed Olive (Bean and Spinach Salad with Olives)

1-1/2 c. dried navy beans, rinsed
1/4 c. olive oil
1 yellow onion, finely chopped
1/2 c. pitted black kalamata olives
1 c. prepared Italian vinaigrette
4 c. spinach, packed, washed, and drained
Salt and pepper to taste
1/2 c. sun-dried tomatoes, chopped
1/2 lb. mozzarella cheese, cubed

Bring a large pot of water to a boil. Place beans in pot, reduce heat, and simmer uncovered 45 minutes. Drain and rinse. Place beans back in pot and add enough water to cover by 3 to 4 inches. Bring to a boil, then lower heat and simmer, uncovered, 45 minutes or until beans are tender but still firm. Drain and rinse beans thoroughly and set aside to cool. Heat olive oil in a skillet over medium heat. Add onion and cook, stirring often, until slightly brown, about 5 minutes. Toss beans, onion, spinach, sun-dried tomatoes, mozzarella, olives, and vinaigrette in a large bowl. Season with salt and pepper. Serve with **Mandolina Pinot Grigio**.

MARGERUM WINE COMPANY/ WINE CASK

After more than 20 years as a restauranteur and wine retailer, Doug Margerum founded Margerum Wine Company in 1999, fulfilling his longtime dream of owning a small-production winery where he could do most of the work himself.

"I wanted to return winemaking to the way it used to be, handcrafted and personal," Doug explains. "My approach is the antithesis of mass production."

Doug has become expert at managing his time—he operates three successful businesses in downtown Santa Barbara's historic Paseo Nuevo: the Intermezzo café (which is the Margerum Wine Company tasting room), the Wine Cask wine shop, and the highly acclaimed Wine Cask restaurant.

And for the past 30 years, Doug has traveled the world, tasting nearly every style of wine produced in every wine-growing region. "I have many points of reference," he says. "Drawing on my tasting experience, I am able to make wine that meets the high standards of my models."

Wine critics are in agreement: *Wine Spectator* magazine notes that "Doug Margerum is proving he has a deft touch as a winemaker," and the *Del Mar Times* praises Doug's varietals as "artisan wines, made for people who know and appreciate wine as it is meant to be."

Doug considers himself a *garagiste*—the term originated in Bordeaux and refers to vintners who make small amounts of high-quality wines, usually in their home garages. Doug's winemaking space is much smaller than a garage: He operates Margerum Wine Company in a 240-square-foot space behind another local winery. Doug concentrates on Rhône-style wines, including M5, a blend of five principal Rhône-grape varieties grown in Santa Barbara County—Syrah, Grenache, Mourvèdre, Cinsault, and Counoise.

"M5 is a complex, elegant expression of wine, an amalgamation of memories of Rhône wines I've tasted and loved over the past 30 years," says Doug.

Doug also makes wine under the Wine Cask label. Aficionados can taste Margerum and Wine Cask wines at Doug's Intermezzo café, a lounge, bar, and light-foods establishment adjacent to the Wine Cask wine shop and restaurant.

Margerum Wine Company/Wine Cask
813 Anacapa Street
Santa Barbara, CA 93101
P. O. Box 23011
Santa Barbara, CA 93121
(805) 966-9463
(800) 436-9463 toll free
doug@margerumwinecompany.com
www.margerumwinecompany.com

Sub-AVA: Santa Ynez Valley

Owner: Douglas Margerum

Tasting Hours:
11 a.m. – 3 p.m. Saturday – Sunday

Wines: Sauvignon Blanc, M5 Rhône-style blend, Syrah, Grenache, Mourvèdre, Counoise, Cinsault

Winemaker's Specialty: Single-vineyard Syrah

Winemaker: Douglas Margerum

Duo of Santa Ynez Fallow Venison

5 lbs. fallow venison short ribs, with short loin attached
2 carrots, diced
2 stalks celery, diced
1 onion, diced
1 *bouquet garni* (ingredients below)
1 bottle Margerum M5 wine
1-1/2 c. veal stock
Salt and pepper to taste
Grape-seed oil to taste
1/2 c. high-quality bitter chocolate, grated

1 stick cold butter
1/2 lb. Telicherry peppercorns

Bouquet garni
3 juniper berries
1-1/2 cloves
1 star anise
2 whole allspice
1/2 cinnamon stick
2 cloves garlic

Season venison with salt and pepper. Heat grape-seed oil in a Dutch oven and sear meat on all sides until golden. Debone and keep warm. Add vegetables to pot and cook until soft and caramelized. Add salt and pepper, *bouquet garni*, meat, and wine. Heat and deglaze pan with wine. Add stock and cover pot with parchment paper. Bring to a simmer, then place covered pot in a 275° oven for approximately 3 hours. Place peppercorns in a saucepan filled with water, bring to a boil, and simmer until water is half absorbed. Repeat nine times until peppercorns are tender. Set aside. Strain sauce through cheesecloth and return to pot. Reduce sauce by one half. Whisk in chocolate, peppercorns, and butter, making sure not to boil mixture. Serve venison with sauce and **Margerum M5**.
Recipe courtesy Executive Chef Jake Reimer, Wine Cask, Santa Barbara

MELVILLE VINEYARDS & WINERY

"Our wine-growing practices begin with the respect we have for the grape itself, its history, and the land that produces it," explains Ron Melville. With his family, Ron owns Melville Vineyards & Winery, which is known for its 100-percent estate-grown Burgundian and Rhône varietals.

Ron's wine-growing career began in the late 1980s, when his family purchased a 180-acre vineyard planted with Chardonnay, Merlot, and Cabernet Sauvignon in the Knights Valley area of Sonoma County. Ron received on-the-job training in viticulture, cultivation, cloning, and trellising while he received formal instruction in enology at the University of California, Davis.

By the mid-1990s, Ron had become fascinated with Pinot Noir but knew that the fragile varietal needed a cooler climate than the Sonoma area offered. Impressed with the Pinot Noirs being produced in Santa Barbara County, Ron purchased 110 acres on Highway 246 in the Santa Rita Hills near Lompoc and 53 acres in Cat Canyon, two miles north of Los Alamos. He founded Melville Vineyards & Winery in 1996.

With the help of his sons, Brent and Chad, Ron planted 82 acres of Pinot Noir, Syrah, and Chardonnay on the Santa Rita Hills property. They also planted Viognier and Syrah on the Cat Canyon acreage, which is known as Verna's Vineyard. Today, Brent manages Verna's Vineyard while Chad handles the Santa Rita Hills estate vineyard.

Melville winemaker Greg Brewer employs a minimalist winemaking style. "I try to remove myself as much as possible from the winemaking process so the honesty and purity of the vineyard can shine through," says Greg. "I use conservative amounts of new oak barrels and transfer wine by gravity and by hand and with short hoses instead of pumping the wine through a machine."

Melville's stately stucco tasting room with a red-tile roof features a fireplace, full kitchen, barrel room, and garden patio with trellised wisteria. Spring wildflowers growing among the vine rows adjacent to the patio create a spectacular sight, adding to the ambience of one of the most elegant wineries in the Santa Rita Hills.

Melville Vineyards & Winery
5185 East Highway 246
Lompoc, CA 93463
(805) 735-7030
melvillewine@cox.net
www.melvillewinery.com

Sub-AVA: Santa Rita Hills

Owners: The Melville family

Tasting Hours:
11 a.m. – 4 p.m. daily

Wines: Chardonnay, Viognier, Pinot Noir, Syrah

Winemaker's Specialties: Chardonnay, Pinot Noir

Winemaker: Greg Brewer

Duck Breasts with Lavender and Pinot Noir

2 duck breasts, boned and cut in half
1 tsp. white-wine Worcestershire sauce
1 tsp. lavender
2 pinches red pepper flakes, divided
1 tsp. ground ginger, divided
2 shallots, thinly sliced and divided
1/2 c. Pinot Noir
1-1/2 c. chicken stock
1 tsp. honey
1 tsp. chopped fresh tarragon
1 Tbsp. butter, at room temperature
1 tsp. cooking oil
Salt and freshly ground pepper to taste

Mix Worcestershire sauce, lavender, and half of the pepper flakes, ginger, and shallots in a small bowl. Rub on duck breasts, cover, and marinate in the refrigerator for 1 to 4 hours. Place wine, stock, remaining pepper flakes, shallots, and ginger in a large skillet and bring to a boil. Reduce heat to a simmer and reduce liquid by one half. Add honey and tarragon and simmer a few minutes longer. Remove from heat and whisk in butter and salt and pepper. Cover and keep warm. Heat skillet to medium heat and add oil. Season duck with salt and pepper and cook 4 to 6 minutes per side until browned and medium rare. Slice breasts and pour reduction sauce over all. Serve with **Melville Pinot Noir**.

MOSBY WINERY

Bill Mosby has always loved biology: "As a kid, I was constantly looking at something under the microscope, from the organisms in pond water to the insects that lived in our back yard," he recalls.

When Bill was a freshman studying pre-dentistry at Oregon State University, he became intrigued with the ancient key to winemaking—the process of fermentation. At his grandmother's farm, he fermented his first batch of juice—to make apple jack wine—setting in motion a lifelong interest in the chemistry of wine that would one day lead to the founding of his own winery.

After graduation from dental school, Bill moved from Oregon to Lompoc to establish a dental practice. "In California, I could make wine from grapes," Bill explains. "That was what I'd been waiting for. I thought I was in heaven!"

Bill became one of Santa Barbara County's pioneer vintners in the early 1970s, when he purchased 250 acres of the historic Rancho de la Vega in Buellton and planted a 45-acre vineyard. He founded Mosby Winery with the intent of producing classic varietals.

In 1985, on a trip to Italy, Bill became inspired by the Italians' passion for winemaking. During the plane flight home, Bill had an epiphany: "I knew I had to make Italian varietals," he explains. "The country's enthusiasm for wine had rubbed off on me."

Soon, Bill began producing only Italian varietals at Mosby Winery. At a friend's winery in Italy, he also made a special varietal, Montepulciano, at a friend's winery in Italy, which he plans to import to the United States and sell at the winery.

Internationally acclaimed artist Robert Scherer creates the labels for Mosby's Artist Series wines, designing an original composition for each wine. Mosby's labels have won numerous awards, including "Best of Show" in all 11 categories of the Orange County wine label competition.

The Mosby tasting room is located in Rancho de la Vega's restored carriage house, which dates from the 1850s and stands adjacent to the vineyard. The ranch was a favorite stopping place for travelers en route from Santa Barbara to San Luis Obispo at the end of the 19th century.

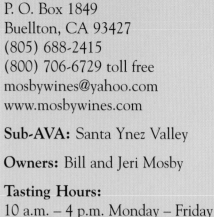

Mosby Winery
9496 Santa Rosa Road
P. O. Box 1849
Buellton, CA 93427
(805) 688-2415
(800) 706-6729 toll free
mosbywines@yahoo.com
www.mosbywines.com

Sub-AVA: Santa Ynez Valley

Owners: Bill and Jeri Mosby

Tasting Hours:
10 a.m. – 4 p.m. Monday – Friday
10 a.m. – 5 p.m. Saturday – Sunday

Wines: Sangiovese, Pinot Grigio, Dolcetto, Teroldego, Lagrein, Cortese

Winemaker: Bill Mosby

Ginny's Tuscan-Style Rabbit

1 rabbit, cut into 5 pieces
Salt and pepper to taste
1/4 c. olive oil
1 yellow onion, thinly sliced
3 cloves garlic, minced
2 bay leaves
1 large sprig rosemary
1 Tbsp. fresh thyme, chopped
2 Tbsp. sugar
1 Tbsp. flour
1/3 c. white-wine vinegar
1 14-oz. can beef broth

1/2 c. dried cherries (or raisins)
Teroldego or other good-quality red wine
1 c. pearl onions
Italian parsley, chopped
1/3 c. pine nuts, toasted

Season rabbit generously with salt and pepper and brown in oil in a heavy skillet over medium-high heat. Remove and keep warm. In the same skillet, sauté onion until soft, about 6 minutes. Add garlic and sauté 1 minute more. Add rabbit to skillet with any juices, along with bay leaves, rosemary, thyme, sugar, flour, vinegar, broth, and cherries. Stir to coat the rabbit pieces. Cover skillet tightly and place in a 350° oven. Braise 30 minutes and stir. If dish seems dry, add a splash of wine. Braise 30 to 50 minutes more until tender. Ten minutes before rabbit is done, add onions and salt and pepper and remove rosemary and bay leaves. Sprinkle with parsley and pine nuts and serve over polenta with **Mosby Teroldego**.

PRESIDIO VINEYARD & WINERY

In 2005, Presidio Vineyard & Winery became the first 100-percent-certified Biodynamic® grape grower in Santa Barbara County. Biodynamic® regulations require very specific measures to strengthen the life processes in the soil and assure that the grapes and wine are free from man-made chemicals. No herbicides, pesticides, or artificial additives may be used during production and processing or in the final bottling of the wine.

Presidio Winery owner Doug Braun believes that stringent organic wine-growing methods not only protect the environment and the consumer but also produce pleasing, distinctive wines.

"Over the years, we've found that using chemical fertilizers leads to unbalanced wines with undesirable aromatics," Doug explains. "At Presidio, we use composts to create a healthy and more balanced soil that accentuates the desirable aromatics of the fruit."

Doug's interest in wine began when he lived in the San Diego area, where he worked as a restaurant manager and graduated in food service management from Grossmont College. Later, Doug earned a degree in enology at California State University, Fresno, and a viticulture degree from the University of California, Davis.

After college, Doug traveled throughout Europe, studying traditional winemaking techniques. Eager to apply Old World principles to the new technologies of wine production, Doug returned to the United States and polished his skills at several small California wineries.

In 1991, Doug began an independent winemaking operation, founding Presidio Vineyard & Winery in Fallbrook to produce affordable Chardonnay and Merlot with purchased grapes. Three years later, Doug moved the winery to Santa Barbara County, where he leased a vineyard.

Presidio acquired its own land in 1999, 100 acres in the cool climate west of the Santa Rita Hills. An advocate for growing varietals in their preferred environment, Doug planted a 30-acre estate vineyard in 2001, dividing his acreage among Pinot Noir, Chardonnay, Syrah, and Viognier.

"The vineyard's proximity to the ocean and the fog that regularly blankets the area creates the perfect conditions for producing the cool-climate varietals Presidio is known for," says Doug.

Presidio Vineyard & Winery
1603 Copenhagen Drive #1
Solvang, CA 93463
(805) 693-8585
(888) 930-9463 toll free
info@presidiowinery.com
www.presidiowinery.com

Appellation of Origin:
Santa Barbara County

Owner: Douglas Braun

Tasting Hours:
11 a.m. – 6 p.m. daily

Wines: Chardonnay, Viognier, Pinot Noir, Syrah

Winemaker's Specialties:
Pinot Noir, Syrah

Winemaker: Douglas Braun

Smoked-Salmon Pasta

2 oz. smoked Coho salmon steak, broken into
  1-inch pieces
1 bag ziti pasta, cooked
3 cloves garlic
3 Tbsp. olive oil
1/2 c. port
12 oz. marinara sauce
1 12-oz. jar fire-roasted red peppers
3 Tbsp. sugar
1/4 c. corn syrup
8 oz. Alfredo sauce
2 Tbsp. Cajun Creole seasoning

1 tsp. cayenne pepper
Black pepper to taste
1 6-oz. can chopped black olives
1 bunch fresh basil leaves

Sauté garlic in olive oil. Add port and marinara sauce. Blend red peppers in blender with sugar and corn syrup. Add to pan. Add Alfredo sauce, Cajun seasoning, cayenne pepper, black pepper, and black olives and simmer 15 minutes. Add salmon and noodles. Garnish with basil leaves and serve with **Presidio Pinot Noir**.

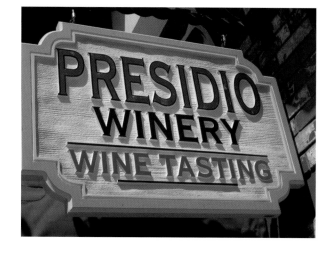

RANCHO SISQUOC WINERY

Eighteen miles east of Santa Maria, a country road weaves past lush pastures, cultivated fields, and fruit orchards to the historic Rancho Sisquoc Winery. Part of an 1852 Spanish land grant, the rancho was named "Sisquoc"—the Chumash word for "gathering place"—more than 150 years ago. Today, Rancho Sisquoc is a gathering place for wine lovers who come to taste the winery's current releases and experience the beauty of Old California.

In 1952, San Franciscan James Flood, a descendant of 19th-century Nevada silver baron James Clair Flood, purchased the 37,000-acre Rancho Sisquoc cattle ranch and farm. The climate and soil reminded him of Sonoma and Napa, and in 1968 he planted a nine-acre vineyard, planning to make wine and sell surplus grapes to other wineries. A rustic-style tasting room was built beside the original, early-1900s farmhouse and barn. The vineyard had its first crush in 1972, and five years later Rancho Sisquoc became a bonded winery.

Just down the road from the winery, on a bluff high above the entrance road, stands San Ramon Chapel. The small wood church was built by Englishman Frederick Wickenden in 1875, at the request of his wife, Ramona Foxen Wickenden (the daughter of English sea captain William Benjamin Foxen, for whom Foxen Canyon Road

and the nearby Foxen Winery & Vineyard are named). Frederick Wickenden purchased the redwood lumber for the chapel and his home with money from the sale of 5,000 head of sheep that he drove from Santa Barbara County to Redwood City. Ramona Wickenden's chapel has been designated an official historic landmark and is pictured on the label of Rancho Sisquoc vintages.

Rancho Sisquoc's vineyard now comprises 310 acres in the easternmost portion of the Santa Maria Valley, near the banks of the Sisquoc River. The winery produces Pinot Noir, Syrah, and Bordeaux-style wines, and continues to supply grapes to many top California wineries.

Rancho Sisquoc Winery
6600 Foxen Canyon Road
Santa Maria, CA 93454
(805) 934-4332
sisquoc@ranchosisquoc.com
www.ranchosisquoc.com

Sub-AVA: Santa Maria Valley

Owners: The Flood family

Tasting Hours:
10 a.m. – 4 p.m. Monday – Thursday
10 a.m. – 5 p.m. Friday – Sunday

Wines: Chardonnay, Sauvignon Blanc, Riesling, Cabernet Sauvignon, Merlot, Syrah, Sangiovese

Winemaker's Specialties: Sylvaner, Pinot Noir, Malbec, Red Meritage, Super Tuscan-style blends

Winemaker: Alec Franks

Redwood-Grilled Salmon

1 fresh salmon filet, skin on (<u>Note</u>: If only skinless salmon filets are available, place on a bed of thickly cut onions on top of wood to grill—see below.)
Olive oil
Fresh garlic, minced
Salt and pepper to taste
1 1-inch by 8-inch piece of rough-sawed redwood, cut to length of filet and soaked in water for half a day
Lemon wedges

Place salmon, skin side down, on wood. Rub filet lightly with olive oil and fresh garlic and season with salt and pepper. Pre-heat grill until hot, then place wood with salmon on grill. Turn heat to low and cover grill. Grill until salmon is done, approximately 30 minutes. Remove wood and salmon from grill. Using a spatula, remove fish from wood, leaving skin attached to wood. Serve with lemon wedges and **Rancho Sisquoc Pinot Noir**.

RIDEAU VINEYARD

At Rideau Vineyard guests can enjoy an array of Rhône varietals while being treated to old-fashioned Southern hospitality in a beautifully restored 1884 adobe. The Alamo Pintado Adobe that once served as a stagecoach stop, an inn, and headquarters for both a dude ranch and a working cattle operation is frequently the scene of lively Cajun-style events hosted by Louisiana-born winery owner Iris Rideau.

Iris is a former investment banker and insurance broker from Los Angeles who in 1990 fell in love with the Santa Ynez Valley while attending a wine festival. She purchased five acres on Alamo Pintado Road in Solvang and built a weekend home and future retirement residence. But in 1995 Iris' retirement plans changed when she became intrigued with the abandoned adobe that stood on a 25-acre parcel next door.

"I thought the building had 'possibilities,'" Iris remembers.

She purchased the property with the intent of converting the historic building into a bed and breakfast. When she learned that zoning restrictions prohibited inns but allowed wineries, Iris changed course. "I was bitten by the winemaking bug," she says, and in 1997 she founded Rideau Vineyards.

Iris restored the Alamo Pintado Adobe to its former glory and furnished it with Victorian antiques, area rugs, and Mardi Gras-style beads and mementos that hang on the walls and reflect her New Orleans heritage. Display shelves house Rideau Vineyards' wine awards and offer visitors wine accessories and Southern-style gourmet packaged foods. Large windows provide impressive views of the vineyards, well-kept lawns, oak trees, wisteria, and gardens of roses and irises.

Rideau Vineyard is the perfect place for picnics, weddings, winemaker dinners, and special events that feature Creole cuisine and music. Iris often showcases her family recipes and cooking skills at her famous Creole Open House, preparing gumbo, jambalaya, and crab cakes for guests to sample with selected wines.

Rideau Vineyard's elegant adobe tasting room and its inviting gardens are a "must-see" for wine tasters.

Rideau Vineyard
1562 Alamo Pintado Road
Solvang, CA 93463
(805) 688-0717
rideauvineyard@verizon.net
www.rideauvineyard.com

Sub-AVA: Santa Ynez Valley

Owner: Iris Rideau

Tasting Hours:
11 a.m. – 5 p.m. daily

Wines: Syrah, Viognier, Mourvèdre, Roussanne, Grenache, Tempranillo, Pinot Noir, Chardonnay, Burgundian-style wines

Winemaker's Specialty:
Rhône varietals

Winemaker: Andrés Ibarra

Iris' Famous Crawfish Étouffée

2 lbs. crawfish tails (available in 1-lb. frozen packages at gourmet markets)
1 to 2 Tbsp. Creole seasoning (to taste)
1/4 c. vegetable or olive oil
1/2 brown onion, finely chopped
1/2 green bell pepper, finely chopped
6 to 8 cloves garlic, finely chopped
3/4 bunch parsley, finely chopped
2 to 3 16-oz. cans tomato sauce (to taste)
6 bay leaves
White rice
Lemon wedges

Drain crawfish, reserve liquid, and place crawfish on a flat tray, sprinkling with Creole seasoning. Sauté crawfish in a skillet until light brown. Remove, set aside, and cover with foil. Heat oil in skillet and sauté onion over medium heat until transparent. Add bell pepper and cook for 10 minutes, until light brown. Slowly add garlic and parsley and cook 10 minutes. Add tomato sauce one can at a time. Simmer a few minutes and add bay leaves and reserved crawfish liquid. Cover skillet and simmer 20 to 30 minutes. Add crawfish and simmer 5 to 10 minutes. Do not overcook. Serve over white rice and garnish with lemon wedges. Serve with **Rideau Viognier** or **Tempranillo**.

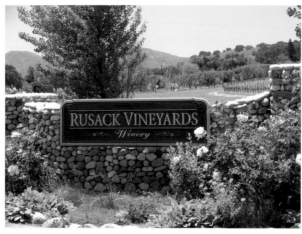

RUSACK VINEYARDS

When Geoff Rusack and his wife, Alison Wrigley Rusack, entered the wine business in the mid-1990s, they had several goals, including growing grapes in the desirable climate of Ballard Canyon in the Santa Ynez Valley and producing world-class wines.

Geoff was an aviation-law attorney and Alison worked in the consumer products division of Walt Disney Company. The couple say they "took a leap of faith" when in 1992 they purchased 48 acres of oak-studded land with an existing 40-acre vineyard in Ballard Canyon and founded Rusack Vineyards. Two years later, they moved with their young family from Los Angeles to a home on the vineyard property.

Geoff and Alison handled all aspects of the business, from crushing grapes to pouring wine in the tasting room, which opened in 1997.

In 2003, the Rusacks replanted 17 acres of the vineyard with vines specifically suited for the Ballard Canyon *terroir*, establishing small, separate blocks that could be individually managed. Vines were planted along the contours of the land in a north/south direction, which allows equal sun exposure for both sides of the canopies and ensures optimal ripening.

Husband-and-wife winemakers John and Helen Falcone make Rusack's award-winning wines with estate fruit and with grapes grown in select vineyards in the Ballard Canyon area.

"We purchase fruit from growers who use custom-farming techniques to meet our standards of high quality," says John.

Rusack Vineyards' wine label features an image of a ceramic tile, inspired by Alison's great-grandparents, who established a handcrafted ceramics factory on Santa Catalina Island in the early 1900s. The tile is symbolic of the care, quality, and creativity that go into all Rusack wines.

The tasting room features a redwood deck built around four enormous oak trees and beautifully landscaped gardens. Rusack Vineyards is one of the most enchanting places to wine taste in Santa Barbara County and the perfect spot for picnicking and enjoying the views of Ballard Canyon's vineyards and hills.

Rusack Vineyards
1819 Ballard Canyon Road
Solvang, CA 93463
(805) 688-1278
info@rusackvineyards.com
www.rusackvineyards.com

Sub-AVA: Santa Ynez Valley

Owners: Geoff and Alison Rusack

Tasting Hours:
11 a.m. – 5 p.m. daily

Wines: Chardonnay, Sauvignon Blanc, Pinot Noir, Syrah, Sangiovese, "Anacapa" Bordeaux blend

Winemakers:
John Falcone, winemaker
Helen Falcone, assistant winemaker

Butternut Squash Soup

1-1/2 lbs. butternut squash, seeded
  and cut lengthwise
7 Tbsp. unsalted butter, melted
1/4 tsp. nutmeg
1/4 c. chopped celery
1/4 c. chopped onion
2 ripe pears, peeled and diced (or 4 canned
  pear halves, diced)
Salt to taste
1-3/4 c. chicken stock
1-3/4 c. water
Fresh sage, chopped and toasted

Chopped walnuts, toasted
Crumbled blue cheese

Brush squash with 2 Tbsp. butter and sprinkle with nutmeg. Place cut sides up on a baking sheet and cover with aluminum foil. Bake at 450° for 1 hour or until squash is soft. Remove from oven, set aside, and cool. Pour 1 Tbsp. butter in a medium skillet. Add celery, onions, pears, and salt, and cook over medium heat until vegetables are soft but not browned, about 5 minutes. Set aside. Heat stock and water in a large pot. Scoop squash flesh from skin and place in pot. Add vegetable-pear mixture and simmer 15 minutes. Heat remaining butter in a small skillet over low heat, stirring often until nut brown; set aside. Puree squash mixture in small batches and stir in browned butter. Ladle soup into individual serving bowls and top with sage, walnuts, and blue cheese. Serve with **Rusack Chardonnay**.

SANFORD WINERY & VINEYARDS

"Always put quality first, because quality is the only thing that endures" is the credo of Sanford Winery & Vineyards, one of the oldest wineries in Santa Barbara County. In 1971, Sanford became the first winery to plant Pinot Noir vines in the Santa Rita Hills area, on a plot of land prized for what winemaker Steve Fennell calls "its magical combination of climate and soil conditions similar to the Burgundy region of France."

"We have produced some of the best and most distinctive Pinot in the world," Steve explains. "Our Pinot is wonderfully aromatic, its flavors plush yet structured with lively acidity and ripe tannins."

Sanford's two estate vineyards, Sanford & Benedict and Rancho La Rinconada, are both located in the Santa Rita Hills, which became an official sub-AVA in 2001. The Sanford Winery team led the effort to establish the new sub-AVA and is proud to have been "instrumental in putting Santa Barbara County and the Santa Rita Hills sub-AVA on the map of the world's great wine regions."

Sanford's wines are made in what is believed to be the largest handcrafted adobe structure built in California since mission days. Completed in 2001, the winery is located on the historic Rancho La Rinconada and is constructed of more than 180,000 adobe bricks hand made on site by Sanford employees. The Mission Revival-style winery requires no air conditioning or heating—the 30-inch-thick walls create an ideal insulation system that

maintains a year-round temperature of 55 to 65 degrees, the perfect environment for wine production.

Sanford adorns its wine bottles with original artwork by nationally known artist Sebastian Titus. Since 1981, Titus has created for Sanford's varietals more than 60 labels, each depicting colorful wildflowers that grow in the Santa Rita Hills. Titus' paintings can be seen on posters for sale within the winery and in galleries and museums across the United States.

Sanford Winery & Vineyards
5010 Santa Rosa Rd.
Buellton, CA 93427
(805) 688-3300
(800) 426-9463 toll free
office@sanfordwinery.com
www.sanfordwinery.com

Sub-AVA: Santa Rita Hills

Owner: Terlato Wine Group

Tasting Hours:
11 a.m. – 5 p.m. daily
(Except some holidays)

Wines: Pinot Noir, Chardonnay, Pinot Noir-Vin Gris, Pinot Grigio, Sauvignon Blanc

Winemaker's Specialty: Pinot Noir

Winemaker: Steve Fennell

Juniper Quail

4 1-lb. quail, quartered, with ribs and
   breast-bones removed
Salt and freshly ground black pepper, to taste
1-1/2 Tbsp. unsalted butter
1/2 Tbsp. light olive oil
2 Tbsp. parsley, finely chopped
1/3 c. fat-free beef broth
1/3 c. Pinot Noir
1 tsp. juniper berries, minced or crushed
2 Tbsp. unsalted butter, softened

Season quail quarters with salt and pepper. Heat butter and olive oil over medium-high heat in a heavy, large frying pan. Add quail, skin side down. Cook and turn occasionally until brown on both sides, with breasts medium rare inside (about 3 minutes) and leg pieces well done (about 6 minutes). Arrange on serving plates. Sprinkle with parsley. Remove excess oil and any burned (not brown) particles in pan. Add broth and wine to pan and cook and stir over high heat until reduced to 1/4 cup. Reduce heat to medium. Add juniper berries and butter and cook and stir until smooth and slightly reduced. Spoon over quail. Serve with wild rice and **Sanford Pinot Noir**.

SANTA BARBARA WINERY

The Volstead Act of 1920 brought an end to commerical wine production in Santa Barbara County. After Prohibition finally ended in 1933, nearly three decades elapsed before the county's winemaking tradition was reestablished—by a Canadian architect about to embark on a lifetime passion for wine.

Born in Montreal, Pierre Lafond moved to Santa Barbara in the late 1950s and ran his family's downtown retail liquor store. Pierre's customers regularly inquired about the availability of locally produced wines, which had been nonexistent since the beginning of the nation's dry years.

In 1962, Pierre was inspired by a group of friends known as "the Mountain Drivers"—local home winemakers famous for their high-spirited harvest festivals—and founded Santa Barbara Winery on Anacapa Street two blocks from the beach. The county's first commercial winery since the end of Prohibition, Santa Barbara Winery began by purchasing grapes to produce "affordable" wines that were sold at Pierre's liquor store.

As Pierre continued to refine his talents as a vintner, he discovered he could make exceptional wines from grapes grown in the fertile soils of Santa Barbara County. In 1972, he purchased land and planted a vineyard in the Santa Rita Hills region just north of the Santa Ynez River. Pierre expanded his winemaking operation in the late 1990s when he built a new winery on the south side of the river, planted another vineyard, and launched a second label, Lafond Winery & Vineyard.

Santa Barbara Winery
202 Anacapa Street
(805) 963-3646
(800) 225-3633 toll free
wine@sbwinery.com
www.sbwinery.com

Sub-AVA: Santa Rita Hills

Owner: Pierre Lafond

Tasting Hours:
10 a.m. – 5 p.m. daily

Wines: Pinot Noir, Syrah, Chardonnay, Sauvignon Blanc, Zinfandel, Cabernet Sauvignon, Riesling, blends

Winemaker's Specialties:
Pinot Noir, cool-climate Syrah

Winemaker: Bruce McGuire

Santa Barbara Winery creates a wide selection of vintages from grapes harvested from its own vineyards and from sourced grapes grown in the cool climates of western Santa Barbara County. Pierre's winery also makes wines using a variety of interesting but lesser-known varietals such as Negrette, Lagrein, and Primitivo.

After nearly four decades of offering his customers award-winning wines, the former Canadian architect is pleased that his Santa Barbara Winery has a reputation as "the hometown winery folks can be proud of." Pierre has enjoyed "the creative process of crafting and bringing things to fruition"— whether a building or a bottle of wine.

Dijon Rack of Lamb

1 rack of lamb (8 or 9 chops)
2 Tbsp. white cornmeal
2 tsp. fresh rosemary leaves, minced
2 cloves garlic, minced (not pressed)
1/2 tsp. coarse kosher salt
Freshly ground black pepper
2 Tbsp. Dijon mustard

Combine cornmeal, rosemary, garlic, salt, and pepper in a bowl and mix well. French the rack of lamb by cutting away meat from the thin ends of the bones. Trim excess fat, leaving enough for flavor. Coat top and sides of rack with mustard, then coat mustard with cornmeal mixture. Place rack of lamb on a baking sheet and roast at 400° for 25 to 45 minutes depending on size of rack and desired doneness. Slice and serve immediately with **Santa Barbara Winery Cabernet Sauvignon** or **Syrah**.

SHOESTRING WINERY

"We started our winery on a shoestring," says Roswitha Craig, who with husband Bill founded the small, family-operated Shoestring Winery in 1999.

The Craigs moved to Santa Ynez from their native Maryland in 1996 to escape the harsh climate. Bill owned and trained thoroughbred racehorses that ran on the East Coast thoroughbred racing circuit and operated a seasonal seafood restaurant with Roswitha from April to October.

"We always loved food and wine and it was our longtime dream to grow our own grapes and make wine," says Roswitha.

Ironically, Bill and Roswitha purchased a former thoroughbred horse ranch on East Highway 246, where they planted Merlot, Sangiovese, Syrah, and Pinot Grigio vines. They built a winery and a tasting room inside the property's 9,000-square-foot barn, whose gravely concrete floor is inlaid with round sections from tree trunks to give horses proper traction.

"The floor is perfect for keeping the winery cool," Roswitha says.

Bill and Roswitha hired winemaker Norm Yost, a 20-year winemaking veteran with an enology degree from the University of California, Davis. Most Shoestring wines are blends made from grapes grown in the Craigs' estate vineyard and from fruit purchased locally.

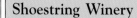

Shoestring Winery
800 East Highway 246
Solvang, CA 93463
P. O. Box 1478
Santa Ynez, CA 93460
(805) 693-8612
(800) 693-8612 toll free
info@shoestringwinery.com
www.shoestringwinery.com

Sub-AVA: Santa Ynez Valley

Owners: Bill and Roswitha Craig

Tasting Hours:
10 a.m. – 5 p.m. daily

Wines: Pinot Grigio, Sangiovese, Syrah, Cabernet Sauvignon

Winemaker: Norm Yost

"Bill and I decide which wines we want to blend together, then we let Norm take it from there," explains Roswitha. "Norm has a very minimalist winemaking style."

All red wines are aged for two years in French oak barrels. "We feel it is really important to give the wine the time to age in the barrels," says Roswitha. "It softens it. We think it's an important step that you can't cut short."

Bill and Roswitha invite visitors to picnic on Shoestring's expansive lawns, to unwind in the shade of the mature trees that grow on the property, or to say hello to Jewels, the Craigs' cutting horse, who keeps a watchful eye on goings-on from his corral near the winery.

Crowd-Pleaser Appetizer

1 loaf marbled rye bread, cut into 1-inch slices
Italian mascarpone cheese, at room temperature
Fresh figs, thinly sliced
Prosciutto, sliced into strips
Fresh mint leaves

Cut bread slices into 2-inch squares. Spread each square with mascarpone cheese and layer with a strip of prosciutto, a slice of fig, and one or two mint leaves. Secure with toothpicks. Serve at room temperature with any **Shoestring** wine.

STOLPMAN VINEYARDS & WINERY

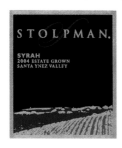

Since the early 1980s, Palos Verdes attorneys Tom and Marilyn Stolpman have attended the Napa Valley Wine Auction to purchase wine for their personal cellar collection. They became inspired to learn about viticulture when they met the vintners and winemakers who produced the vintages they loved to collect.

In the late 1980s, the Stolpmans decided to become wine growers. They embarked on an extensive search for property that had the ideal soil and climate necessary to grow exceptional grapes. They acquired 220 acres in Ballard Canyon and, in 1990, founded Stolpman Vineyards. The couple purchased the land for its maritime climate and unusual soil—a stratum of limestone underlies two feet of clay.

"The make-up of the ground offers a rare opportunity for producing fine wine," explains Tom. "The shallow topsoil and the pH of the limestone stresses the vines, creating optimum growing conditions."

The Stolpman estate vineyard was developed in several phases: 102 acres were planted from 1992 to 1995, and 60 acres from 1999 to 2000. Today the vineyard totals 180 acres, with 80 percent planted to Syrah.

"From the time we planted the first vineyard in '92, we have been continually experimenting to find what varietals grow best in our microclimate," Tom says. "We know now that our area is the perfect place for Rhône varietals and Sangiovese."

The couple established Stolpman Vineyards to grow fruit to sell to wineries and to provide grapes for small batches of wine Tom planned to make for family and friends. When Tom realized that his customers were making award-winning wines with Stolpman grapes, he increased his own wine production, creating Stolpman's first commercial vintage in 1997.

In 2001, Tom hired Italian enologist and international wine consultant Alberto Antonini and winemaker Sashi Moorman, who employs a minimal-interventionist winemaking style. Sashi created Stolpman's "La Croce," a blend of 50 percent Syrah and 50 percent Sangiovese—the two varieties are harvested together and co-fermented in the same new French oak barrels in which they are then aged for 18 months.

Stolpman Vineyards & Winery
1659 Copenhagen Drive, Suite C
Solvang, CA 93463
(805) 688-0400
info@stolpmanvineyards.com
www.stolpmanvineyards.com

Sub-AVA: Santa Ynez Valley

Owners:
Tom and Marilyn Stolpman

Tasting Hours:
11 a.m. – 5 p.m. daily

Wines: Syrah, Sangiovese, Roussanne

Winemaker's Specialty: "La Croce" Syrah and Sangiovese blend

Winemaker: Sashi Moorman

Grilled Marinated Leg of Lamb

1 4-1/2- to 5-lb. boneless leg of lamb, butterflied and trimmed of fat
1/2 c. Stolpman extra-virgin olive oil
1/4 c. fresh lemon juice
4 cloves garlic, minced
1 Tbsp. dried oregano, crumbled
2 tsp. salt and 1 tsp. black pepper
Cantaloupe slices

Combine olive oil, lemon juice, garlic, oregano, salt, and pepper in a 2-gallon zip-lock bag. Add lamb, seal bag and turn to coat lamb with marinade. Place in a shallow pan and refrigerate for at least 8 hours, turning bag over occasionally. Bring lamb to room temperature about 1 hour before grilling. Remove from bag and discard marinade. Insert 4 or 5 skewers to prevent meat from curling when cooked. Grill on a lightly oiled rack, over direct medium-high heat, turning occasionally until medium rare or until thermometer registers 125° to 128°. (Note: Close lid if using gas grill.) Transfer lamb to a cutting board and remove skewers. Cover lamb loosely with foil and let stand about 20 minutes or until internal temperature reaches 135°. Cut across the grain into slices and serve with cantaloupe and **Stolpman Estate Syrah**.

SUMMERLAND WINERY

Wine critics have given Summerland Winery rave reviews since its founding: *Dan Berger's Vintage Experiences* praises the winery's offerings as "superb wine from a new producer," *Wine Enthusiast* magazine deems Summerland "the real deal," and *Robert M. Parker, Jr.'s The Wine Advocate* wants to know, "Who are these people?"

The people are Nebil "Bilo" Zarif and Kevin Bening, who established Summerland Winery in 2002 to produce a diverse range of premium wines and small lots of vineyard-designated Pinot Noir.

Turkish-born Bilo developed an affinity for wine—particularly the wines of Bordeaux, Burgundy, and the Rhône Valley—while attending school in Paris. When he moved to the United States, he traveled to Napa, where he visited premier wineries and purchased several reserve wines for his collection. As he learned more about California wines, Bilo decided to forge a career in the wine industry and produce varietals from the diverse growing regions of the Central Coast.

In the late 1990s, Bilo formed a partnership with San Luis Obispo County's Laetitia Vineyard & Winery and Barnwood Vineyards. Several years later, he sold his interest in the wineries and founded Summerland Winery, which opened its tasting room doors in the town of Summerland in 2004.

Summerland Winery bottles wines under two labels, the Central Coast Collection and the reserve Single Vineyard Collection. Both labels are made with grapes grown in the coastal region reaching from Monterey County to Santa Barbara County.

"Wines in the Central Coast Collection are blended in a fruit-forward style and are excellent for food pairing," explains Bilo. Describing his Single Vineyard Collection, he says, "We put in a lot of miles traveling the region tasting wines and meeting with growers before a vineyard site is selected. Our reserve tier comprises single-vineyard bottlings from top vineyards that express the distinct *terroir* of each site."

All Summerland wines are blended under the guidance of Bordeaux winemaker and consultant Michele Pignarre le Danois. Michele visits the Summerland Winery several times a year to choose barrels, taste wine, and confer with resident winemaker Etienne Terlinden.

Guests can sample Summerland's current offerings in the tasting room or on the terrace that offers bistro tables and a view of the Pacific Ocean.

Summerland Winery
2330 Lillie Avenue
Summerland, CA 93067
(805) 565-9463
info@summerlandwine.com
www.summerlandwine.com

AVA: Central Coast

Owner: Nebil "Bilo" Zarif

Tasting Hours:
11 a.m. – 5 p.m. Monday – Thursday
11 a.m. – 7 p.m. Friday – Sunday

Wines: Pinot Gris, Sauvignon Blanc, Viognier, Chardonnay, Orange Muscat, Pinot Noir, Syrah, Petite Sirah, Merlot, Cabernet Sauvignon

Winemaker's Specialties: Chardonnay, Pinot Noir, Rhône-style blends

Winemaker: Etienne Terlinden

Grilled Allspice Short Ribs

5 lbs. Angus beef short ribs, boned
Kosher salt and freshly toasted ground
   black pepper to taste
1/2 c. grape-seed oil
1-1/2 medium onions, sliced
2 carrots, diagonally sliced
2-1/2 stalks celery, diagonally sliced
3/4 c. garlic cloves, peeled
1 c. tomato paste
1 bottle Summerland Merlot

1/2 Tbsp. ground cinnamon
1 tsp. ground allspice
1 tsp. whole cloves
2 bay leaves
1 qt. veal stock
1/2 bunch each Italian parsley and thyme, chopped
1 Tbsp. peppercorns

Season beef with salt and pepper. Heat grape-seed oil in a Dutch oven over medium-high heat. Brown meat, remove, and keep warm. Add vegetables and garlic to pot and cook until caramelized and brown. Add tomato paste and wine. Cook over medium heat until slightly thickened, stirring to scrape browned bits from the bottom of the pan. Add remaining ingredients and meat and bring to a simmer. Cover and bake in oven at 400° until fork tender, approximately 2 to 2-1/2 hours. Remove from oven, strain cooking liquid, and pour over meat. Refrigerate overnight. Barbeque or charbroil over medium-high heat. While meat is cooking, reheat cooking liquid, reduce to sauce consistency, and season with salt and pepper. Spoon sauce over meat and serve with **Summerland Merlot.**
Recipe courtesy Chef Troy Tolbert, Wine Cask, Los Olivos

SUNSTONE VINEYARDS & WINERY

"Our goal was to create a place where wine and food could be enjoyed in a picturesque atmosphere," says Linda Rice, who with husband Fred and their children—Bion, Brittany, and Ashley—own Sunstone Vineyards & Winery. One of the most beautiful wineries in the Santa Ynez Valley, Sunstone resembles a small Provençal winery in the French countryside.

In 1989, the Rice family moved from Santa Barbara to Santa Ynez and purchased a 55-acre horse ranch, where they planted Rhône and Bordeaux varietals. In 1994, the Rices converted a barn on the property into a winery and founded Sunstone Vineyards & Winery.

Several years later, heavy winds from a rainstorm caused an oak tree to fall on the winery, damaging it beyond repair. The family constructed a new French-style winery, which includes two tasting bars, a gourmet kitchen, an elegant 5,000-square-foot barrel-aging cave with chandeliers and a fireplace, and an inviting courtyard patio set among lavender and rosemary.

Since its inception, Sunstone has grown its grapes without using herbicides, pesticides, or fungicides. In 1994, the California Certified Organic Farmers association approved the 77-acre vineyard as 100 percent organic.

"The CCOF certificate is one of the toughest to get," explains Ashley, Sunstone's operations manager. Bion, president of Sunstone, emphasizes the advantages of organic wine growing: "Not only do organic vineyards and toxin-free soils more accurately reflect the Santa Ynez Valley *terroir*—avoiding chemical use benefits the health of our customers and the people working here. Our goal is to capture the true essence of this vineyard in your glass."

Sunstone's specialty wine is the acclaimed "Eros," a Bordeaux-style blend named after the Greek god of love. The wine label, an original work by internationally known artist James Paul Brown, shows a man and woman exchanging a kiss. Sunstone suggests pairing Eros with portobello mushrooms, filet mignon, or, for an "ecstatic" flavor experience, dark chocolate.

Sunstone Vineyards & Winery
125 Refugio Road
P. O. Box 1747
Santa Ynez, CA 93460
(805) 688-9463
(800) 313-9463 toll free
club@sunstonewinery.com
www.sunstonewinery.com

Sub-AVA: Santa Ynez Valley

Owners: The Rice family

Tasting Hours:
10 a.m. – 4 p.m. daily

Wines: Viognier, Chardonnay, Merlot, Cabernet Franc, Syrah, Sauvignon Blanc, blends

Winemakers' Specialty:
"Eros" Bordeaux-style blend

Winemakers:
Daniel Gehrs, Brittany Rice

Purple Potatoes with Oven-Dried Tomatoes and Goat Cheese

6 purple potatoes, sliced to 1/4-inch thickness
Olive or grape-seed oil
4 Roma tomatoes, sliced paper thin
Salt and pepper to taste
4 to 8 oz. goat cheese, at room temperature
Basil for garnish, finely chopped

Sprinkle tomatoes lightly with salt. Place on greased or parchment-lined baking sheet. Drizzle with oil and sprinkle with salt and pepper. Bake at 150° to 200° for 20 to 30 minutes, until dried. Set aside. Place potatoes on a greased or parchment-lined baking sheet. Drizzle with oil. Bake at 350° for about 8 to 10 min, until soft but not soggy. Place potatoes on individual serving plates and top each slice with a dried tomato slice. Spoon a dollop of cheese on top and sprinkle with basil. Serve with **Sunstone Rapsodie Du Soleil**.
Recipe courtesy Chef Brittany Rice

WHITCRAFT WINERY

"Winemaking is a marriage between art and technology," says Whitcraft Winery owner Chris Whitcraft, a 30-year winemaking veteran who earned degrees in music, political science, and pre-law before becoming a producer of fine Burgundian-style wines.

Chris became interested in wine in the 1970s when as a student he worked for several retail liquor stores and a specialty wine shop. He had planned to become a lawyer, but just before entering law school he realized his real interest was winemaking. He quickly changed course, immersing himself in the study of wines—he took enology classes at the University of California, Davis, read numerous wine publications, regularly tasted a variety of wines, and volunteered at several Northern California wineries.

In 1985, Chris founded Whitcraft Winery and became a wholesale wine distributor; a labeler who designed wine labels for restaurants and country clubs; and a *negociant-eleveur*—a wine merchant who buys lots of fermented wines, blends them, and bottles them for sale under private labels.

When he founded Whitcraft, Chris knew the varietals he wanted to produce.

"I was extremely driven to make quality, Burgundian-style wines that I wouldn't be afraid to drink myself," he explains. "My wines are unique, fuller and richer because of the way I *don't* process them."

Grape clusters are hand sorted and foot crushed, then placed in a basket press to extract the remaining juice. No chemicals or enzymes are added to the wine and almost no electricity is used in production—wines are moved by gravity flow from one vessel to another and are never pumped, fined, or filtered.

Chris' artistic talent is evident in the Whitcraft label that pictures four palm trees growing in the shape of a "W," with a Chardonnay leaf as background. Chris designed the label as a tribute to his first Whitcraft wine and to recall "The Big W" in the 1960s comedy hit "It's A Mad, Mad, Mad, Mad World." The movie that featured the tall, slanting palms was filmed in Santa Monica, Palos Verdes, and Long Beach, near the beaches where Chris surfed as a youth.

Whitcraft Winery
36-A South Calle Cesar Chavez
Santa Barbara, CA 93103
(805) 730-1680
whitcraftwinery@cox.net
www.whitcraftwinery.com

AVA: Central Coast

Owner: Chris Whitcraft

Tasting Hours:
Noon – 4 p.m. Friday – Sunday

Wines: Chardonnay, Pinot Noir, Syrah, sparkling wine

Winemaker's Specialty: Pinot Noir

Winemaker: Chris Whitcraft

Bacon, Pork, and Sausage Cassoulet

1/2 c. diced bacon
1 lb. lean pork, cut into bite-size pieces
1/2 lb. smoked sausage, skinned and sliced
Salt and pepper to taste
3 Tbsp. flour
8 oz. tomato sauce
1/2 c. sliced carrots
1/2 c. diced onion
1/2 c. diced celery
1/2 c. diced red pepper
4 cloves garlic, chopped
1 15-oz. can diced tomatoes

1 serrano pepper (or other hot pepper), chopped
2 c. chicken broth
2 15-oz. cans white beans, well rinsed
Fresh thyme, oregano, parsley, and bay leaves to taste

Sautee bacon in a large Dutch oven until rendered. Add pork and sausage and cook thoroughly, stirring often. Season with freshly ground pepper. Remove meat to a bowl. Add flour to fat in pot and whisk. Cook and whisk over medium heat until almost peanut-butter brown. Add tomato sauce and stir. When mixture is bubbling, add vegetables and cook until almost soft. Add tomatoes. When bubbling add chopped pepper, broth, and beans. Cook until bubbling and stir in meat and salt. Cover pot and bake at 375° for 1 hour. Serve with **Whitcraft Pinot Noir**.

ZACA MESA WINERY & VINEYARDS

Founded in 1972, Zaca Mesa Winery & Vineyards is one of Santa Barbara County's pioneering vintners of the post-Prohibition era and in 1978 became the first area wine grower to plant Syrah. Zaca Mesa president Brook Williams explains that at the winery, which is dedicated to the production of Rhône varietals, "We grow everything we make and make everything we grow."

All Zaca Mesa wine comes from grapes grown on its 750-acre property, which lies in the northern portion of the Santa Ynez Valley, an area of hills and high mesas that rose from the valley floor millions of years ago. The terrain is rugged and only 242 acres of Zaca Mesa's land is suitable for planting—the estate vineyard grows on a mesa 1,500 feet above sea level.

"The nearly flat mesa allows for uniformity and consistency from vine to vine," says Brook, "and the rocky soil is well drained, which promotes vigorous growth and intensely flavored grapes."

The mesa vineyard enjoys warm sunny days with cool, breezy afternoons and evenings. Brook emphasizes

that "this combination of the near-perfect temperature and soil conditions has created an environment ideal for growing Rhône varietals."

The majority of the winery's prized Syrah vines grow on rough terrain similar to the wine-producing land found in the Rhône region of southern France. Zaca Mesa's well-known Black Bear Block Syrah is made from fruit grown in "Mesa H," the original Syrah vineyard planted in 1978.

Guests are invited to sample Zaca Mesa's wines in the sunlit tasting room, or in the adjacent patio and garden, where they can play a game of chess on a ten-foot-square chessboard. Visitors are also encouraged to hike on the trails that lead to an extraordinary view of the Santa Ynez Valley.

Zaca Mesa Winery & Vineyards
6905 Foxen Canyon
P. O. Box 899
Los Olivos, CA 93441-0899
(805) 688-9339
info@zacamesa.com
www.zacamesa.com

Sub-AVA: Santa Ynez Valley

Owners: The Cushman family

Tasting Hours:
10 a.m. – 4 p.m. daily (All year)
10 a.m. – 5 p.m. Fri. – Sat. (Summer)

Wines: Syrah, Viognier, Roussanne, Chardonnay, Rhône blends

Winemaker's Specialty: Syrah

Winemaker: Clay Brock

Grilled Tri-Tip Oso Negro

1 2- to 2-1/2-pound tri-tip roast
8 cloves garlic, chopped
1/4 c. olive or vegetable oil
1 Tbsp. salt
1/2 tsp. whole black peppercorns
1/4 tsp. ground cumin
1/4 tsp. dried oregano leaves
1/4 tsp. dried sage leaves

Mix the garlic, oil, salt, peppercorns, cumin, oregano, and sage in a blender. Process until mixture becomes a coarse paste. Score the fat layer of the tri-tip with a sharp knife, cutting just through the fat and not into the meat. Put the tri-tip in a large zip-lock plastic bag along with the garlic paste, seal it, and work the garlic paste into the meat until the meat is evenly coated on all sides. Marinate at room temperature for 1 to 2 hours. Prepare grill with hot coals on one side of barbeque. Place the tri-tip on the grill, fat side down, directly over the coals. Sear the meat on both sides for 3 to 4 minutes per side. Move meat to the other side of grill in indirect heat. Place the lid over the barbeque and open all vents. Cook to desired doneness and slice against the grain. Serve with **Zaca Mesa Black Bear Block Syrah**.
Recipe courtesy Theresa V. Laursen, cookbook author

Foxen Cyn Road

↑ LOS ALAMOS 1

MEMBER OF WINE INSTITUTE

Historic El Camino Real

CENTRAL COAST VINEYARD TEAM

PROMOTING SUSTAINABLE VINEYARD PRACTICES

Member

SANTA Ynez VALLEY WINE COUNTRY

RUSACK VINEYARD ▲

◄ LOS OLIVOS VINTNERS LOS OLIVOS

◄ ARTHUR EARL LOS OLIVOS

SUNSTONE VINEYARD & WINERY ►

◄ STOLPMAN VINEYARDS SOLVANG

BUTTONWOOD FARM WINERY ►

◄ LUCAS & LEWELLEN VINEYARD SOLVANG

◄ RIDEAU VINEYARDS

◄ PRESIDIO WINERY SOLVANG

KALYRA WINERY ►

◄ DANIEL GEHRS WINES

◄ ROYAL OAKS WINERY SOLVANG

CHARDONNAY LN

BALLARD CYN RD

Los Olivos
POP 1,000   ELEV 825

Foxen Canyon Wine Trail

COTTONWOOD
CAMBRIA
BYRON
RANCHO SISQUOC
FOXEN
BEDFORD THOMPSON
ANDREW MURRAY
FESS PARKER
CURTIS
FIRESTONE

Santa Ynez
POP. 4,200   ELEV. 550

California Certified Organic Farmers
CCOF
Certified — California — Organic — Farmers
Certified Grower

Organically grown in accordance with the California Organic Foods Act of 1990

Wine country signs

"Old wine and friends improve with age." — Italian proverb

Fall foliage at Koehler Winery

"A bottle of wine contains more philosophy than all the books in the world."
— Louis Pasteur, French chemist and microbiologist (1822-1895)

The Rancho Los Alamos Vineyard at Alisos Canyon Road and Highway 101, Los Alamos

"What is better than to sit at the end of the day and drink wine with friends?"
— James Joyce, expatriate Irish writer and poet (1882-1941)

California poppies bloom beside Alamo Pintado Road just south of Los Olivos.

Page 132: Wildflowers planted in the vineyard at Curtis Winery in Los Olivos make for a brilliant June display.

"Wine is the most healthful and most hygienic of beverages."
— Louis Pasteur, French chemist and microbiologist (1822-1895)

"Let us have wine and women, mirth and laughter,
Sermons and soda-water the day after." — Lord Byron, British poet (1788-1824)

A bucolic scene along Santa Rosa Road in Buellton

"A book of verses underneath the bough. A jug of wine, a loaf of bread, and thou."
— Edward FitzGerald, English writer and poet (1809-1883)

"Give me women, wine and snuff
Until I cry out 'Hold, enough!'"
— John Keats, English poet (1795-1821)

Ballard Canyon Road, Solvang/Los Olivos

MORE WINE–TASTING VENUES

The following listings include several local wine shops and and an inn offering additional settings for visitors to enjoy wines from a variety of Santa Barbara County wineries that do not maintain their own tasting rooms.

BALLARD INN TASTING ROOM

Ballard Inn Tasting Room
2436 Baseline Avenue
Ballard, CA 93463
(805) 688-7770
(800) 638-2466 toll free
innkeeper@ballardinn.com
www.ballardinn.com
Tasting Hours:
Noon – 5 p.m. Friday – Saturday

Featured Wineries:

Ken Brown Wines
(805) 688-4482
ken@kenbrownwines.com
www.kenbrownwines.com
Owners: Ken and Deborah Brown
Wines: Chardonnay, Pinot Noir, Syrah,
Winemaker's Specialty: Pinot Noir
Winemaker: Ken Brown

Kenneth-Crawford Wines
(805) 693-1340
info@kennethcrawford.com
www.kennethcrawford.com
Owners: Kenneth J. Gummere,
Mark Crawford Horvath
Wines: Grenache, Syrah, Pinot Noir
Winemakers' Specialties:
Cool-climate Syrah and Pinot Noir
Winemakers: Kenneth J. Gummere,
Mark Crawford Horvath

Vandale Vineyards
(805) 688-0255
vanwine@silcon.com
Owner: Beth Vandale
Wine: Sangiovese
Winemaker: Bruno D'Alfonso

CELLAR 205 WINERY & MARKETPLACE

Cellar 205 Winery & Marketplace
205 Anacapa Street
Santa Barbara, CA 93101
(805) 962-5857
christina@cellar205.com
www.cellar205.com
Tasting Hours:
11 a.m. – 5 p.m. daily

Featured Wineries:

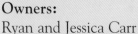

Alchemy Wine Productions
(805) 245-0753
nic@alchemywineproductions.com
www.alchemywineproductions.com
Owner: Nicolas Donahue
Wines: Chardonnay, Syrah
Winemaker's Specialty: Syrah
Winemaker: Nicolas Donahue

Carr Vineyards & Winery
(805) 455-7271
info@carrwinery.com
www.carrwinery.com
Owners:
Ryan and Jessica Carr
Wines: Pinot Gris, Pinot Noir, Syrah, Cabernet Franc
Winemaker's Specialties: Pinot Noir, Cabernet Franc
Winemaker: Ryan Carr

Oreana Winemaking Company
(805) 962-5857
christian@cellar205.com
www.oreanawinery.com
Owner: Christian Garvin
Wines: Sauvignon Blanc, Verdelho, Pinot Noir, Syrah, sparkling wine
Winemaker's Specialties: Verdelho, Pinot Noir
Winemaker: Christian Garvin

LOS OLIVOS TASTING ROOM & WINE SHOP

Los Olivos Tasting Room & Wine Shop
2905 Grand Avenue
Los Olivos, CA 93441
(805) 688-7406
pinotgrigio@verizon.net
www.losolivoswines.com
Tasting Hours: 11 a.m. – 6 p.m. daily

Featured Wineries:

Brophy Clark Cellars
(805) 929-4830
info@brophyclarkcellars.com
www.brophyclarkcellars.com
Owners: John Clark,
Kelley Brophy Clark
Wines: Sauvignon Blanc,
Pinot Noir, Syrah, Zinfandel
Winemaker's Specialty: Pinot Noir
Winemaker: John Clark

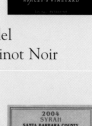

J. Kerr Wines
(805) 688-5337
jkwines@msn.com
www.jkerrwines.com
Owners:
John and Joan Kerr
Wines: Chardonnay, Syrah, Zinfandel
Winemaker's Specialty: Chardonnay
Winemaker: John Kerr

Ojai Vineyard
(805) 649-1674
info@ojaivineyard.com
www.ojaivineyard.com
Owners:
Adam and Helen Tolmach
Wines: Chardonnay, Viognier, Pinot Noir,
Syrah
Winemaker's Specialty: Syrah
Winemaker: Adam Tolmach

OLD MISSION WINE COMPANY

Old Mission Wine Company
1539 Mission Drive
Solvang, CA 93463
(805) 686-9323
honeywood@verizon.net
www.oldemissionwinecompany.com
Tasting Hours:
9:30 a.m. – 5:30 p.m. Sunday – Thursday
9 a.m. – 6 p.m. Friday – Saturday

Featured Wineries:

Labyrinth Wine Cellars
(805) 268-4155
ajhill@labyrinthwine.com
www.pinotnow.com.au
Owner: Ariki Hill
Wine: Pinot Noir
Winemaker: Ariki Hill

Michael Grace Wines
(805) 291-1008
info@michaelgracewine.com
www.michaelgracewine.com
Owners: Michael and Grace McIntosh
Wines: Cabernet Sauvignon, Syrah, Grenache, Rhône-style blends
Winemaker's Specialty: Grenache
Winemaker: Michael McIntosh

Three Saints Vineyard
(805) 693-0744
info@threesaintsvineyard.com
www.threesaintsvineyard.com
Owner: James Dierberg
Wines: Chardonnay, Pinot Noir, Syrah, Merlot, Cabernet Sauvignon
Winemaker's Specialty: Merlot
Winemaker: Nicholas de Luca

William James Cellars
(805) 478-9412
robin@williamjamescellars.com
www.williamjamescellars.com
Owners: Jim and Robin Porter
Wines: Chardonnay, Roussanne, Syrah, Grenache, Grenache Rosé, Pinot Noir, Cabernet Sauvignon, Cabernet Franc, port
Winemaker's Specialty: Syrah
Winemaker: Jim Porter

TASTES OF THE VALLEYS

Tastes of the Valleys
1672 Mission Drive
Solvang, CA 93463
(877) 622-9463 toll free
info@tastesofthevalleys
www.tastesofthevalleys.com
Tasting Hours:
11 a.m. – 10 p.m. daily

Featured Wineries:

Arcadian Winery
(805) 688-1876
joe@arcadianwinery.com
www.arcadianwinery.com
Owner: Joseph Davis
Wines: Chardonnay, Pinot Noir, Syrah
Winemaker's Specialty: Pinot Noir
Winemaker: Joseph Davis

Au Bon Climat
(805) 937-9801
info@aubonclimat.com
www.aubonclimat.com
Owner: Jim Clendenen
Wines: Chardonnay, Pinot Noir,
Pinot Blanc/Pinot Gris blend
Winemaker: Jim Clendenen

Lane Tanner Winery
www.lanetanner.com
Owner: Lane Tanner
Wines: Pinot Noir, Syrah
Winemaker's Specialty:
Pinot Noir
Winemaker: Lane Tanner

Qupé Wine Cellars
(805) 937-9801
info@qupe.com
www.qupe.com
Owners:
Bob and Louisa Lindquist
Wines: White Rhône-style varietals, Syrah
Winemaker's Specialty:
"Bien Nacido Hillside" Estate Syrah
Winemaker: Bob Lindquist

WINE COUNTRY

Wine Country
2445 Alamo Pintado Avenue
Los Olivos, CA 93441
(805) 686-9699
sales@syvwinecountry.com
www.syvwinecountry.com
Tasting Hours: 11 a.m. – 5 p.m. daily

Featured Wineries:

Core Wine Company
(805) 598-5050
becky@corewine.com
www.corewine.com
Owners: David and Becky Corey
Wines: Grenache Blanc, Roussanne,
Marsanne, Syrah, Grenache, Mourvèdre
Winemaker's Specialties:
Mourvèdre, Grenache
Winemaker: David Corey

Dierberg Vineyard
(805) 693-0744
info@dierbergvineyard.com
www.dierbergvineyard.com
Owner: James Dierberg
Wines: Chardonnay, Pinot Noir
Winemaker's Specialty: Pinot Noir
Winemaker: Nicholas de Luca

Fiddlehead Cellars
(800) 251-1225 toll free
info@fiddleheadcellars.com
www.fiddleheadcellars.com
Owner: Kathy Joseph
Wines: Sauvignon Blanc, Pinot Noir
Winemaker's Specialty: "Fiddlestix
Vineyard Cuvée Lollapalooza" Pinot Noir
Winemaker: Kathy Joseph

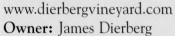

Flying Goat Cellars
(805) 688-1814
ynot@flyinggoatcellars.com
www.flyinggoatcellars.com
Owners: Norm and Pam Yost
Wines: Pinot Gris, Pinot Noir,
Sparkling Rosé de Noir
Winemaker's Specialty:
"Goat Bubbles" sparkling wine
Winemaker: Norm Yost

**Great Oaks Ranch &
Vineyard**
(805) 686-0895
nancy@greatoaksranch.com
www.greatoaksranch.com
Owner: Nancy Lippman
Wines: Sauvignon Blanc,
Syrah, Bordeaux-style blends
Winemaker's Specialty:
"Windmill Hill Cuvée"
Winemaker: Andrew Murray

J. Wilkes
(805) 899-2845
info@jwilkes.com
www.jwilkes.com
Owners: Jeff and Kimberly Wilkes
Wines: Pinot Blanc, Pinot Noir
Winemaker's Specialties:
"Bien Nacido Vineyard" Pinot Noir,
Solomon Hills Vineyards Pinot Noir
Winemaker: Jeff Wilkes

Silver Wines
(805) 963-3052
benjamin@silverwine.com
www.silverwine.com
Owner: Benjamin R. Silver
Wines: Viognier, Syrah,
Pinot Noir, Cabernet
Sauvignon, Nebbiolo, Sangiovese,
Cabernet Franc, Mourvèdre
Winemaker's Specialty:
"I Tre Figli" ("The Three Sons") blend
Winemaker: Benjamin R. Silver

Star Lane Vineyard
(805) 693-0744
info@dierbergvineyard.com
www.starlanevineyard.com
Owner: James Dierberg
Wines: Sauvignon Blanc,
Syrah, Cabernet Sauvignon
Winemaker's Specialty:
Cabernet Sauvignon
Winemaker: Nicholas de Luca

Waltzing Bear Wines
(877) 958-9464 toll free
info@waltzingbearwines.com
www.waltzingbearwines.com
Owner: Brad Lowman
Wines: Viognier, Pinot Noir,
Petite Sirah
Winemaker's Specialty: Pinot Noir
Winemaker: Brad Lowman

GLOSSARY

American oak barrels   Barrels made from oak wood of the species *quercus alba*, from a U.S. forest

Appellation   A name used to designate the official geographic origin of a wine

Balance   The interrelationship of a wine's alcohol, tannin, residual sugar, and acid content

Battonage   The process of stirring wine as it ages on its lees in the barrel

Blend   A wine that is made from two or more lots of wine, usually from the juice of two or more grape varieties

Body   The perceived "weight" or viscosity of a wine in the mouth

Bouquet   The fragrance of a wine, which includes several aromatic elements formed by the oxidation of fruit acids and alcohol

Bung   An apparatus used to seal a container, such as a bottle, tube, or barrel

Calcareous   Of, like, or containing calcium carbonate, calcium, or lime

Character   A tasting term used to describe the flavor elements of a wine that give it substance or integrity

Clone   A sub-variety of a grape variety comprising a group of genetically identical vines propagated asexually from a single vine

Co-fermentation   The process of fermenting two or more varieties of grapes together to make a blended wine. Blends are usually made by combining two or more separately fermented wines.

Cold soak   A pre-fermentation maturation process where crushed grapes are stored at a low temperature to enhance the color of the juice

Dry   The opposite of the term "sweet" when describing wine

Estate wines   Wines that are produced from grapes owned or controlled by the winery

Fermentation   The gradual, natural process that occurs when yeast transforms the sugar in grape juice into alcohol

Fining   To refine or clarify wine

Finish   The taste of the wine that remains in the mouth after it has been swallowed

French oak barrels   Barrels made from oak wood of the species *quercus robur*, from the forests of France, considered the finest type of oak for aging most white wines

Fruit forward   Having the first impression of flavors and aromas suggestive of fruit

Hang time   The time from *vêraison* until the grapes are harvested

Horizontal wine tasting   A side-by-side wine tasting of the same wine varieties

Lees   The natural sediment of grape skins, pulp, and yeast that settle to the bottom of the barrel or vat as a wine ferments and ages. Wines undergo raking to remove these sediments.

Maceration   The contact of the grape skins with the juice to leach the skin's color, tannin, and other substances into the juice

New oak   Oak barrels that are brand-new or that have been used four or fewer times

New World   A collective term applied to winemaking countries located outside Europe

Old oak/neutral oak   Oak barrels at least five years old that have lost most of their oaky character

Old vine   A term for a vine whose fruit is deemed exceptional due to the vine being, generally, at least 40 years old and producing a low-yield crop

Old World   A collective term for the winemaking countries of Europe

Phylloxera   A parasite that attacks the roots of grapevines, causing the death of the plant

Pomace   The pulp of grape-skin and grape-seed residue

Punching down   Breaking up grape-skin caps and other solids during red wine fermentation

Raking   Moving wine from one barrel to another in order to separate it from settled solids—the lees—at the bottom

Regulated deficit irrigation (RDI)   An irrigation-management technique that limits water to stress vines, reducing fruit quantity and thereby increasing fruit quality

Reserve   A wine deemed finer than the normal version of the same wine

Rootstock   A root in which a graft is inserted for propagating plants. Specific rootstocks are chosen for disease and pest resistance as well as for soil conditions.

Single-vineyard wine   A wine made from the grapes of one vineyard that usually displays the name of the vineyard on its label

Structure   The interaction of a wine's alcohol, acid, tannin, and sugar components, which contribute to its texture and feel in the mouth

Sur lie   A wine that has aged on its lees in the barrel

Tannin   A flavor component derived from grape seeds, stems, and skins. Oak barrels also contain tannin.

Terroir   A French term used to describe the growing conditions in a vineyard, including soil, drainage, exposure, climate, microclimate, and other factors that make a site unique

Transverse valley   A valley lying on an east/west axis, with one end opening to the ocean

Varietal   A wine named for the grape variety from which it was made

Varietal character   The characteristics of a specific grape variety

Vêraison   The change from berry growth to berry ripening in grapevines

Vertical wine tasting   A side-by-side wine tasting of wines of the same variety from the same winery that are sequenced by vintage

Vinification   The process of making wine

Vintage   The year in which a wine's grapes grew and were harvested

Viticulture   The process of growing grapes

Yeasts   One-celled microorganisms that grow quickly in a liquid containing sugar, responsible for transforming grape juice into wine

RECIPE INDEX

WHERE TO STAY

The author provides the following list of accommodations for the convenience of visitors to Santa Barbara County's wine country. The listing does not constitute an endorsement of any particular establishment. Guests are encouraged to visit the Web sites or contact the proprietors before making reservations.

SANTA MARIA

Historic Santa Maria Inn
801 South Broadway
Santa Maria, CA 93454
(805) 928-7777
(800) 462-4276 toll free
www.santamariainn.com

SANTA YNEZ VALLEY

Edison Street Inn
1121 Edison Street
P.O. Box 1718
Santa Ynez, CA
(805) 693-0303
www.edisonstreetinn.com

Fess Parker's Wine Country
  Inn & Spa
2860 Grand Avenue
Los Olivos, CA 93441
(805) 688-7788
(800) 446-2455 toll free
www.fessparker.com

Santa Ynez Inn
3627 Sagunto Street
P. O. Box 628
Santa Ynez, CA 93460
(805) 688-5588
(800) 643-5774 toll free
www.santaynezinn.com

SOLVANG

The Ballard Inn
2436 Baseline Avenue
Solvang, CA 93463
(805) 688-7770
(800) 638-2466 toll free
www.ballardinn.com

The Inn at Petersen Village
1576 Mission Drive
Solvang, CA 93463
(805) 688-3121
(800) 321-8985 toll free
www.peterseninn.com

Marriott Santa Ynez Valley
555 McMurray Road
Buellton, CA 93427
(805) 688-1000
(800) 638-8882 toll free
www.marriott.com

Meadowlark Inn
2644 Mission Drive
Solvang, CA 93463
(805) 688-4631
(800) 344-9792 toll free
www.meadowlarkinnsolvang.com

Solvang Gardens Lodge
293 Alisal Road
Solvang, CA 93463
(805) 688-4404
(888) 688-4404 toll free
www.solvanggardens.com

Storybook Inn
409 First Street
Solvang, CA 93463
(805) 688-1703
(800) 786-7925 toll free
www.solvangstorybook.com

SANTA BARBARA

Bath Street Inn
1720 Bath Street
Santa Barbara, CA 93101
(805) 682-9680
(800) 341-2284 toll free
www.bathstreetinn.com

Brisas del Mar, Inn at the Beach
223 Castillo Street
Santa Barbara, CA 93101
(805) 966-2219
(800) 468-1988 toll free
www.sbhotels.com

Casa Del Mar Inn
18 Bath Street
Santa Barbara, CA 93101
(805) 963-4418
(800) 433-3097 toll free
www.casadelmar.com

Cheshire Cat Bed & Breakfast
36 West Valerio Street
Santa Barbara, CA 93101
(805) 569-1610
www.cheshirecat.com

Colonial Beach Inn
206 Castillo Street
Santa Barbara, CA 93101
805-963-4317
800-649-2669 toll free
www.sbhotels.com

The Eagle Inn
232 Natoma Avenue
Santa Barbara, CA 93101
(805) 965-3586
www.theeagleinn.com

Four Seasons Resort The Biltmore
  Santa Barbara
1260 Channel Drive
Santa Barbara, CA 93108
(805) 969-2261
(800) 819-5053 toll free
www.fourseasons.com/santabarbara

Inn by the Harbor
433 W. Montecito Street
Santa Barbara, CA 93101
(805) 963-7851
(800) 626-1986 toll free
www.sbhotels.com

James House Santa Barbara Bed &
  Breakfast
1632 Chapala Street
Santa Barbara, CA 93101
(805) 569-5853
www.jameshousesantabarbara.com

The Orchid Inn at Santa Barbara
420 West Montecito Street
Santa Barbara, CA 93101
(805) 965-2333
(877) 722-3657 toll free
www.orchidinnatsb.com

White Jasmine Inn
1327 Bath Street
Santa Barbara, CA 93101
(805) 966-0589
(800) 962-0589 toll free
www.whitejasmineinnsantabarbara.com

RAIL TOURS

For transportation, accommodations, and tour packages to Santa Barbara County wineries, contact:

The Overland Trail
1949 Club Lounge Railway Car
2054 South Halladay Street
Santa Ana, CA 92707
(714) 546-6923
(800) 539-7245 toll free
www.overlandtrail.com

REFERENCES

Research material used in the preparation of this book includes the following:

BOOKS

Ciovacco, Justine, et al., *State-by-State Atlas* (D K Publishing, 2003)

Coombs, Gary B., Anna Dato, and George H. Adams, *Those Were the Days: Landmarks of Old Goleta* (Institute for American Research, 1986)

DeLorme Mapping Company, *Southern & Central California Atlas & Gazette* (DeLorme Publishing Company, 1998)

Geraci, Victor W., *Salud! The Rise of Santa Barbara's Wine Industry* (University of Nevada Press, 2004)

Graham, Otis L., et al., *Aged in Oak* (Santa Barbara County Vintners' Association, 1998)

Hinkle, Richard Paul, *Central Coast Wine Tour from San Francisco to Santa Barbara* (Vintage Image, 1977)

Kramer, Matt, *Matt Kramer's New California Wine* (Running Press, 2004)

McNutt, Joni G., *In Praise of Wine* (Capra Press, 1993)

Millner, Cork, *Vintage Valley* (McNally & Loftin, 1983)

Ribéreau-Gayon, Pascal, *Hachette Atlas of French Wines & Vineyards* (Hachette, 1989)

Teiser, Ruth, and Catherine Harroun, *Winemaking in California* (McGraw-Hill, 1983)

World Book Encyclopedia (World Book Inc., 1990)

GOVERNMENT AGENCY SOURCES

Alcohol and Tobacco Tax and Trade Bureau (U. S. Department of the Treasury)

Santa Barbara County Agriculture Department

WEB SITES

www.britannica.com

www.ca-missions.org/honig.html

www.californiamissons.com

www.en.wikipedia.org

www.independent.com

www.nass.usda.gov

www.santabarbaraca.gov

www.sbcountywines.com

www.staff.esuhsd.org

www.ttb.gov

www.west.net

www.wineinstitute.org

www.winespectator.com

and individual Web sites from all featured wineries